WE CAN

WE CAN

The Executive Woman's
Guide to Career Advancement

Robin Toft

MERACK PUBLISHING

© 2019 by Robin Toft

Toft Group
Attn: Robin Toft
11250 El Camino Real, Ste. 102
San Diego, CA 92130

www.robintoft.com

Published and distributed by Merack Publishing.

Library of Congress Control Number: 2018963694

Toft, Robin (1960-)

WE CAN: The Executive Woman's Guide to Career Advancement

ISBN: 978-1-949635-02-7

Text set in Georgia

Cover design by Jimi Scherer

Printed in the United States of America

*This book is dedicated to my truly exceptional
and inspirational team at Toft Group,
who share my passion for helping mid-career women
maximize their career opportunities and lives.*

*Thank you—I hope you all realize everything
you have dreamed of in this life and more!*

CONTENTS

ACKNOWLEDGMENTS

My first Toft Group employee, Heather Burns, inspired me to create my executive search business and take her with me when I founded my company. We started at zero and we built a very significant company—I always call her the other founder.

I'm exceptionally proud of my partners Angela Brooks, Sarah Cueto, Larry Hansen, Scott Jackson, Raul Lamas, Lisa McCann, Steve Merwin, Tyeara Shelley, Linda Sierra, Mark Soufleris and Rachael Thor who have created Toft Group's exceptional reputation based upon a team-based culture of flawless execution. As we scaled, our Chief Financial Officer, Dorrie Chung, was my right hand in building our executive search firm from early revenue to multi-millions over the first six years. Ron Giannotti, Toft Group's President & Chief Operating Officer, inspired me to write this book and share my wisdom with aspiring professional women everywhere. I'm thankful for the experience, and his enduring commitment to empowering women worldwide.

Dolly Bauer, my personal assistant 25 years ago at my first biotech company, was the first person assigned to me when I walked in the door there. She returned to work for me as Toft Group's San Francisco office manager, and she has created a can do attitude throughout the company, inspiring me and her colleagues daily.

My male mentors along the way helped support me in tough times, and provided unlimited inspiration and guidance. Universally, they bet on me and I didn't let them down. Rich Carter deserves special mention since he gave me my first opportunity in executive search and placed a winning bet on me when I was a cancer patient on a long road to recovery. I will also be forever thankful to Steve Nielson, my first sales leader, who taught me everything I know about sales. I still use his "3 good reasons" technique today. Other significant and seasoned executives in my life included Bob Whelan, Tim Brodnik, Bill Young, Ronnie Andrews,and Heiner Dreismann, the men who believed in me and looked out for me in the board-room. Myla Lai-Goldman remains a special friend and my best female mentor turned CEO, whom I will always admire.

And, of course, I need to thank my mother and father who were always wildly supportive of my big dreams and who infused confidence in me from an early age. Both told me I could do anything in this world, and thankfully I believed it. My father showed me the value of hard work—and set the example for the executive that I aspired to become. I'll be forever grateful for their support and the incredible gift of confidence—the best gift you can give a child.

PROLOGUE

I want to start this journey together with one simple thought: if you are a female executive targeting a role in the C-suite, it's likely that everything you want to do has already been done before.

I'm sure for many of you that is a discouraging concept, one that leaves little room for shattering glass ceilings or blazing new trails. But if we stop for just a moment and really think about what often holds us back from doing what we truly want to do, it's fear of the unknown—the risk of a road less travelled. We worry about what it means to be the one paving a new pathway without a guide. So let's think of this again and shift our mindset. Everything you want to do has already been done before. There is hope in that idea. It means you can do anything you want—it's all possible. And not only is it possible, but we have a road map to make it so by learning from all of the masters that have come before us. By reading the accounts of others or asking the right people for the help we need, we can take the lessons others have learned before us and internalize them.

My hope in writing this book is to be a guide on your road to becoming a powerful female executive. What follows is a set of tools that you can utilize to design and advance the career of your dreams. While I want you to be inspired and motivated by this book, more importantly I want to give you the right language, the sense of value, the resources and the connections that will empower you to turn that inspiration into action. It's time to find—and follow—your passion.

INTRODUCTION

On July 5, 2006 I boarded a plane in San Francisco, headed to Europe for a big officer level meeting at my company's corporate headquarters in Switzerland. The entire executive team came with me to do a roadshow throughout Europe to exhibit our global business product lines and to collaborate with our European business partners to develop product launch strategies for the up and coming commercialization phase of our business.

On the plane, I got sick—I was a shell of a person when I landed. By the time I arrived at my hotel, I could barely walk. I remember washing my clothes by hand in the shower, hanging them to dry, and thinking to myself, *I have to be up in four or five hours for a networking event.*

During that morning's event attended by executives of a large multinational pharmaceutical company, I pretended to be okay. But in reality, I could hardly stand up. One of the only executive women on the white, male-dominated European board came over to me and began sharing her story. She had cancer and was telling me how sick she had been in the months leading up to the diagnosis. At the time, I didn't realize how foretelling our interaction would be—my morning had already mirrored her experience. Little did I know it wouldn't stop there.

Throughout the day I kept thinking to myself, *It's a massive GI illness—the kind that will pass in 24 to 48 hours.*

Strong women who are in control of their universe, their families, and their circumstances typically tend to overlook symptoms or simply write them off because they don't have time to be ill. Once before, I had gone to the doctor due to gastrointestinal distress and was told,

"It's probably nothing—you just changed your diet." In the back of my mind, I knew something was astray, but I just went on with my life and powered through—that is my tendency.

This time was no exception; instead of going to a hospital, I went on with the roadshow. There were five of us in various functions from my business unit, and I was the global commercial operations leader.

From country to country, we informed organizations of our global product launch plans for the coming year, pledged our commitment to them, and gave them reassurance they were in good hands—we would deliver all of their products on time. It was a lot of intensity every day. And every time I ate, I would get sick. But I kept going.

On the second to last day, I called my husband.

"Hey, can you please try to make me a doctor's appointment?" I asked. "The minute I get home I have to go—there is something serious going on here."

But the next day, the last day of the event, something curious happened. At my hotel, I suddenly felt great. *Oh my gosh, I'm completely better.* I called my husband and had him cancel the appointment. A doctor's appointment would take away necessary time, and I was too busy for that—I needed to parachute back into my life and continue to make a bunch of amazing stuff happen.

But the relief didn't last. Soon after I got on the plane and they served the meal, I was sick all over again. This time, it lasted the entire way home.

At this stage in my life, I thought I had everything under complete control: I was commuting 50 miles each way to work within the San Francisco Bay Area (which I later realized was not very healthy), I worked out regularly, ate well, and had what I thought was life balance. To some extent, I had been enjoying my job, but I also found myself increasingly frustrated because I was trying to make significant change happen in a predominantly male European culture. It was stressful, but I didn't realize just how stressful it really was while I was in the thick of it.

Upon landing, I went straight to the emergency room. My little town on the coast of California had a very small, unsophisticated emergency room, and they thought I had developed food poisoning on a 4th of July camping trip right before I left for Europe. Just to be sure, that doctor suggested I go up the road to a larger hospital and get a CT scan.

Twelve hours later, I was working from my laptop in the larger hospital's ER—antsy to get out of there. "Oh good. You're here," I said to the doctor as he entered the room, "When can I get out of here? I have a lot of work to do." The doctor looked at me and in a serious tone said, "You're not going anywhere. You've got colon cancer." He proceeded to tell me that nothing could get through my intestines because the cancer had caused an obstruction, and that I needed emergency surgery.

My husband started crying. I was in disbelief; it was completely beyond my comprehension that this could happen to me. I was always in complete control. I had work-life balance. I knew I had a lot of stress from both the commuting and the job, but surely not enough for this? They had to bring me the lab data showing that my CEA levels were through the roof for me to believe I actually had cancer.

The following morning at six o'clock, I had emergency surgery. They took out 15 inches of my colon and immediately sent me for chemo at UCSF in San Francisco. At that time, the minimum age for a colonoscopy was 50—I was 45 years old.

I don't eat fat. I don't eat meat. I exercise every day—I'm in complete balance. There is no history of colon cancer in my family. How could this happen to me?

The diagnosis shocked me, but I had no choice—I rose to the occasion. This was not going to take me down. Immediately, I knew I had to resign from my job. In my mind, it had contributed to the cancer. I say to people quite frequently, "If you had a life and death experience and you knew you may not survive it, would you quit your job?"

My answer was a definitive "yes." If your answer is "yes," even now as you sit here reading this book, you need to resign from your job. You need to find your way into something that makes you personally happy— genuinely very, very happy.

After resigning, I put my house on the market, staged it beautifully, and it sold immediately. I moved to a mountain in San Diego to recover and every day I climbed that mountain. Every two weeks, my nurses would take the line out of my neck and I'd go to the gym to stay in good physical fitness as I worked through my treatment.

By far, it was not the worst thing that has happened to me in my life, and it was actually quite a learning experience. The ordeal made me be honest and real about what I wanted to do—I knew immediately when I moved to San Diego and lived on the mountain that I wanted to pursue executive search as my career. Putting it off hadn't been the right decision. That was my "A-ha" moment. A boutique executive search firm was what I wanted—not a big, multinational global company like I'd just come out of.

During my quest to find the right executive search company to work for, a recruiter called, seeking to recruit me as an executive.

"No, sorry," I replied. "I'm going into executive search."

"Why don't you come and help me out? I'm leaving my practice unattended. I just bought the whole company—you can manage my San Francisco office."

As you might imagine, that presented a challenge—now in San Diego, living on a mountain, I wasn't exactly in the area. But I agreed to do it remotely and fly there on occasion during my remaining three to four months of chemotherapy.

Even though it wasn't what I had originally intended, this was an opportunity to learn from him while I was recovering.

One year post-cancer, I had learned to allow myself time off and was heading out on a vacation to Antarctica. By the time I reached London, I received a message asking if we were okay in the fires. *What fires?* I wondered.

It was a really scary moment. While I had no idea what they were talking about given that I was out of the country, I soon learned that our house had burned down. Fortunately, my parents were house sitting for us and were able to get my dogs and themselves out safely, which I'm very thankful for. These were the big Southern California wildfires in 2007; we lost absolutely everything. My only possessions left were the cold weather clothes filling the suitcase I had brought on our trip.

The year before, I had already realized that life was not about things. That's a very clear message you understand when you have survived cancer—life is about relationships and people. Physical things will come and go in your life, but people are your world. The greatest outcome of the whole neighborhood burning was the relationships we built—we became exceptionally close friends with all of our neighbors. We all went through this same life-changing experience together, and we all came out the other side happier as a result of what happened.

This really intensified and solidified my pursuit of executive search; I came back, buckled down, and worked even harder to build a relationship business that was continually meaningful to me.

My renewed sense of purpose led me to my ultimate goal: changing the way cancer was treated in my lifetime. The available treatments are very inefficient, difficult, and often cancer-causing themselves because of the chemotherapy and radiation combinations used. With new treatments on the horizon, including cell therapy and immunotherapy, I wanted to be involved by working with the companies developing the products. By finding them great executives, I could help them get their products to market more quickly. In order to do executive search the way I really wanted to, in order to fix what I felt was a broken system, I knew I would need to change everything about the process.

I split off from my semi-remote job on amenable terms to open my own practice in San Diego shortly after the fire. I wanted to work where I lived and embrace the community where I was.

Executive search was a challenging industry—one that most clients disliked as a whole. It was slow. It was difficult. It was often unacceptable to clients in the current framework and because of that, I knew I was going to build a very different executive search firm with Toft Group. One employee came with me and she's still with me today. She was very much the inspiration to venture out on our own and be successful. We started with zero revenue, a handful of customers, and a really good foundation of understanding—we wanted to create something different.

The rest is history. We've grown from zero to approximately $10 million in revenue within eight years and there's no end in sight. The focus in the first ten years was to change the way cancer is treated in our lifetime. The next ten will be about advancing women in their careers. Early on, we took the position that we needed to know every single executive female in the space—we won awards for placing an unprecedented number of women. Within the third year of doing business, we were placing 42 percent women into executive roles. Today we're maintaining that, and we're aiming for 50 percent. Diversity is the answer—I would not be surprised if that percentage grows even further over the next five to ten years. After all, women are 50 percent of the population.

Even today in San Diego's biotech industry, which is cutting edge, innovative, and leading the world in so many respects—we're still very much in the dark on the issue of equality. A 2016 report released by UK-based executive recruitment firm Liftstream found only two percent of companies in this industry had a female CEO. I find it strange that as women we wake up every day, go to work in these companies run by men, and don't question or make a bigger deal of that statistic when—in theory—fifty percent of the leadership team should be women. **Women graduate college with PhDs and Masters at the same rate as men, but they just aren't escalating to the top of these organizations at an equal pace.**

The history of the world—all of it—has been male-dominated. In the United States, women are fortunately able to compete on a *more* level playing field, but even in America there are still major battles to be won. Here the issues are different—but frankly, they're just dressed better and wearing nicer shoes.

One of those issues we're working to find parity on is compensation. To this day, there is still a large discrepancy between what a woman earns and what a man earns.

Sadly, it isn't anything new.

According to Dr. Sundari Anitha from the University of Lincoln and Professor Ruth Pearson from the University of Leeds' website Striking Women, women had no choice but to work during the second half of the 19th and early 20th century in Victorian England. They needed to help support their families and were paid less than their male counterparts who were working alongside them. From the 1850s onward, trade unions began to be established, first among better paid workers and then expanded to represent a wider range of workers. Women, however, remained for the most part excluded from trade unions, and unequal pay was the norm.

Once I started to become more aware—once my eyes were opened to it—I saw evidence of inequality everywhere. It was all around me and has been with us throughout history. I saw it clearly when I traveled internationally and just as prolifically back at home in the United States. Everywhere I looked, there it was: the injustice of the gender wage gap. It was (and still is) a global epidemic.

Even though I hadn't noticed it in my younger years, the gender/wage gap had been there right in front of me all along, silently growing—rooting itself in my own early career as well as in my family history. My mom married at eighteen, had three children by the age of twenty-five, and didn't work outside the home until I was five years old. She joined the workforce as a poorly paid administrative assistant, which was one of only four major career choices available to women at the time: secretary, nurse, teacher, or factory worker. Her choices were limited and, because she was reliant on my dad's income and committed to taking care of her children, she didn't have the ability to leave freely at any given time.

I learned that we as women have to be self-sustaining and self-directed. I grew up believing that I was never going to rely on anyone other than myself. Watching my young mother struggle with three children was enough to make me vow never to be in that situation myself. I made a decision to choose a different path. Everything I wanted to do had been done before, but I did it my own way.

As women, we need to make our own money, but it goes beyond that. We need to invest in ourselves—in our relationships, in our health, and most of all, in our dreams. There is a really important reason why you choose the career that you choose. Dial into that as early as you can. You don't need a near death experience to learn that while you're not in control of every aspect of your life, you do have control over how you show up and how you create the life you want to live.

I have dedicated my life to making a difference for the world and for other people. And it's been the most joyful thing for me to put my focus forward facing rather than on myself. It makes life so much more productive and successful because things come back to you in the volume that you give them.

Now it's your turn.

Take these lessons to heart and work through the steps carefully so that when you put this book down, you're ready. Ready to own your feminine power, to believe in the value you've created, and to advance the career of your dreams.

Let's get started!

DREAMS AND MOTIVATION

The path from dreams to success does exist.
May you have the vision to find it,
the courage to get on to it,
and the perseverance to follow it.

Kalpana Chawla

The "will to live," to me, is a given. We were born with so many gifts and privileges. We're able to read books like this one, and we have so many possibilities that lie in front of us. Life is super exciting! We have the ability to get better every day, make choices about where to go, and how to spend our time.

But the "will to thrive" is the "will to live"—enhanced. It's when you've found your calling on this planet and have crossed the line from just living life to living your best life. How are you really going to make a difference in this world? Significance is one of the greatest human needs. Everybody who is thriving would like to be significant and leave the world a better place. This is when you actually cross the chasm. In the past, you've done a lot of things that other people have wanted you to do, but once you cross over, now it's your turn to decide: it's time to do your passion project.

If on one side is "surviving" and the other side is "thriving," the bridge between the two is choice. Choice is something that is best taught at an early age. My sincere wish is that everyone reading this book teach their children (if they have them) that they can do anything they want in this world—that choice is indeed possible. A lot of people weren't lucky enough to have someone who programmed them with this mindset. My parents didn't go to college and I didn't grow up with a lot of advantages, but they did instill in me the belief that anything is possible. Specifically, my father told me I could be anything I wanted to be in the world. That is the single best gift you can give to a child—a solid foundation and a "can do" attitude.

Without that programming, a person can reach thirty years of age and still not believe in herself. She then has to manufacture that mindset and come up with a belief in herself by sheer choice. And it really does boil down to choice. You have to decide to truly believe you have the power to do whatever you want in this world. You must make a commitment to yourself that you're no longer satisfied just surviving; you really want to thrive and are willing to change to do that. The decision to buy this book was a first step. By reading this book and internalizing it, you will begin to believe that you deserve the life you desire. Feeling you deserve to thrive is a choice you must make and commit to.

I want you to be able to say, "I am worthy of having a good life where I can actually make a difference. I'm here for a purpose." (If, for whatever reason, that belief is lacking for you and you can't instill it in yourself, you might opt to get a professional's help). Please do it. You deserve to have a life that is very rewarding, that exists far beyond just survival. I believe in you. And you should, too.

Being able to say you are worthy of thriving is one thing—knowing and internalizing it is another (which undoubtedly takes longer). Once you truly believe it, you then must hold yourself accountable.

Everyone is here for a purpose—it's your job to discover what that means for you. Start by asking yourself, "Why am I here? What is the difference I can make in this world?" If it's raising amazing children and being the best mom you can be, that's awesome. It may be that in addition to other things. If a career fits into your life plan, commit to figuring out how to make it a career that's meaningful. Emanate goodwill and happiness in all areas of your life—not only for yourself but for everyone else around you.

If becoming a female executive is your goal and what you truly dream of being, ask yourself:

- Does leading a company fall in line with my passions?
- Would it make me happy?
- Are the day-to-day demands and the life of a female executive the way I really want to spend my life?
- What lifestyle do I ultimately desire?

As you work through these questions, allow yourself to close your eyes and envision the life of a female executive to see if it's truly in alignment with the life of your dreams.

Making the life you desire a reality will take a tremendous amount of work and commitment. The power of your dream must be compelling enough to provide you the staying power necessary to go the distance toward its realization.

FINDING YOUR PASSION

Finding your passion involves determining both what you're good at and what you love to do. Up until the moment you realize what you're striving for, you may have been good at everything you did, but none of it was truly enjoyable. All of those jobs and industries were worthwhile, though: you were making footprints along your path to being here. It means getting to a stage in your life where you can say, "I'm going to take all these things that I believe I'm really good at, put them together, and find a job that requires them all." When you reach that place, it won't feel like working. It'll feel like playtime—getting paid for everything you absolutely love to do and thrive on doing.

When you find your career of choice—your passion place—it's like having walked through a garden of freshly fallen snow. When you stop to look back at where you came from, you see every step that you've taken on the journey and every lesson you learned along the way. Maybe you discovered what you're not going to do or decided not to continue down a certain path. Every experience, whether positive or negative is all critically important to a person's growth and development, and at some point it will all make sense. When you discover your passion place and take flight, when your rocket takes off, you're no longer walking through the snow. In that moment, you'll say, "Ahhh. So that's why I needed that experience!" Looking forward, there aren't any more footprints—just fresh snow. You're up in the air, in all senses of the phrase: elevated from your excitement and happiness, with a wide and clear path that leads in many directions. Pursuing your passion place will be that magical. Every day, you'll leap out of bed in the morning and can't wait to hit it hard.

Many women ask, "Why can't I find my passion place sooner? Do I have to wait fifteen, twenty years into my career to discover who I am?" In response I say, "Finding your passion place is a journey. You can't reach your ultimate destination until you know where you want to go. The road is defining your passion project and working toward reaching it. Some fortunate people determine what it is for them very early on, but there is still a road to the realization of that dream. Everyone has their own pace. Someone else's timeline shouldn't define what yours should look like. As long as you always have the yearning to be in your sweet spot, to actually make money doing what you love, you're on the right path. That yearning is a core competency for success."

I have found that many women fail at finding their passion because they simply pursue what they are "supposed" to be good at. Women have a tendency to do what everyone else wants them to do; most are people pleasers. If you end up doing what you're good at but not necessarily what you want to do, don't give up and stay there—just stand back and reassess.

I went through this, too. Doing what everyone expected me to do, I went to college. Although my parents—especially my father—instilled in me a great attitude, I still needed to find my passion for myself. Passion is often hard to find in those early stages. If you allow yourself to be controlled by factors around you, you'll always be weighed down by the expectations of others instead of your own. You'll begin to start placing limits on yourself that you wouldn't have before. This will lead to different life choices and compromise—you'll end up outside of your passion place. But never give up on your goal to be in a job that you love, no matter how long it takes. Work is where we spend so much of our time, we simply need to get it right.

It's never too late.

I didn't go into sales until I was thirty. Julia Child didn't publish her first book until the age of forty-nine. A lot of people don't start running marathons until they're fifty-five.

Although it sounds a bit cliché, sixty truly is the new thirty. I meet people every day of all ages who have remarkable levels of energy and physical health. They all have an ability to make a difference. There isn't a deadline on what age you need to find your passion. I've seen many, many examples of women finding themselves after their children leave for college. The point is to always be preparing and searching for it.

Women can find their passion place and start or return to a career path at any time in their lives. Whether you're first entering the working world fresh out of college or starting a new career trajectory after raising children, it's never too late to pursue career aspirations.

YOUR IDEAL JOB

As an executive search professional/recruiter, there are two questions I love to ask when helping a candidate pinpoint what their next actionable steps are with their career: 1) What is your ideal job? and 2) What are the "must haves" that make up your ideal career choice?

Everyone should be able to answer those two questions for themselves. Maybe not at first—it does take a little bit of exploration—but, in the end, everyone should know the ingredients of their perfect job. Perhaps the "must haves" for you are flexibility in work hours, amazing coworkers and colleagues, a meaningful cause, and a performance-based pay structure. You won't really know until you consciously think about it.

Finding your ideal job does take some trial and error. During our time in school, we may have had no idea what we really wanted to do. We probably had some idea of what we *liked* to learn about, but some of the professions that are the most impactful are not even well-known options.

For example, no one I knew seemed to understand what an executive search professional was or did. At least, no one I spoke to about careers told me about it—hence why I like to call it the best kept secret of occupations. It's an amazing job in which we match executives with their ideal occupations. The people who find executive search, or who happen to make their way into it, learn that it's a really remarkable occupation. There are so many extraordinary professions like that in this world, but first you have to determine what you're good at doing. Then you have to put it all together in a package and ask, "Is there a job that requires all these strengths?"

Someone might say, "I like to take pictures, but photography doesn't pay that well." I urge you to rethink that belief. Many professions use the skill of photography or the skills inherently paired with a knowledge of photography that pay quite well. You have to figure out a way to leverage pay for what you desire to do. Some people don't have high aspirations for compensation, so that wouldn't necessarily be part of their "must have" list, but others definitely care about monetary compensation. It is your job to line up what you can leverage against your "must have" list. That's why you'll want to look inside of yourself first, before you go outside to seek opportunities. Take what is most important to you and match your skills to it. This way, you can craft your perfect career AND make money doing it.

When I first worked in the laboratory setting and realized that everybody was going to earn the exact same amount if they were awesome or not, I was incensed. It was infuriating to me to trade hours for money instead of being rewarded for hard work. I ended up in sales because it is a profession where you make more if you sell more. For me, it was really important that I would be paid in direct proportion to what I contributed. My current occupation as an executive recruiter is also largely compensated with commissions, and it still works very well for me. Figure out what your motivators are, in order of priority, and you'll have one of the main ingredients for your perfect job.

Some common examples of important job ingredients are listed below, but this is not a comprehensive list:

- Experienced leadership team
- Meaningful mission & vision
- Compensation amount and structure
- Geographic location
- Culture committed to work/life balance
- Flexibility of hours and/or commuting

Honestly, that's why a lot of professionals fail in choosing their ideal field—they don't know which ingredients matter most to them and end up unhappy with the work they are doing. A great example I can think of is a newly minted lawyer. Law firms require many long, hard hours of interpersonal interaction, and it's amazing how many people aspire to be attorneys without realizing this. The first or second year post-law school can be a rude awakening for the introvert who has become accustomed to isolated reading and now struggles to acclimate to hours-based billing, challenging meetings, and other intense interactions with many other people.

As you think through what motivates and what works as an incentive for you, you'll begin to get a sense of what's important in a job. After aligning what matters to you with what you're good at doing, take that to your trusted network. Ask knowledgeable people you respect what professions offer that intersection. Once you have an idea of which careers might work for you, go talk to people in those professions and get a reality check: "Is this occupation actually all that I'm thinking it is?"

Let me give you an example. I was well into my professional career as an executive, leading commercial operations and selling things, but I always sensed I belonged in Human Resources (HR). I needed to slow down long enough to go and talk to people who were actually in HR and see if there were any roles in that field that required sales skills. It took me some time to figure out where those two intersected, but I found it in executive search.

Robin's Ideal Job Shortlist:

I absolutely love building relationships, and I love being with customers.

Because of my years of experience in the biotech industry specifically, I wanted to have some aspect of technology and life sciences involved.

I wanted to earn good money (I'd become accustomed to this after my early success in sales, so that was a given).

The amount of money I earned needed to be proportional to how much and how hard I planned to work.

I love selling—especially closing deals; deal-making was a key ingredient for me. Sales is not just about the interpersonal interactions, either. If you only like the interactions and relationships, you could be in customer service or another service-oriented role. For me, I thrive on hunting and closing deals while working closely with people.

I took that intelligence about myself, put it all together, and sought to figure out if there was an occupation that encompassed all of those traits and skills. The list led me to two different careers: Real Estate and Executive Search (which the latter is actually kind of like real estate, but with humans and their careers instead of physical brick and mortar buildings).

The moment I measured my shortlist against these two professions, it was very clear that the field for me was Executive Search. With my science background and the impact I could have on patient lives coupled with my sales skills, mastery of relationship building, and negotiation abilities, I discovered that HR was—and still is—the best place for me.

Recently, the wife of a doctor came to me to discuss her career aspirations. She hadn't worked in seventeen years. This woman was absolutely remarkable on every level. Then, she showed me her resume. She had been taking a night course about clinical trial research—not at all what she'd been doing before.

"Why do you want to pursue this?" I asked. "Your background is perfectly suited to the sales side of medical affairs."

Then we launched into the most amazing conversation. She felt obligated to enter into this type of work because it had been suggested to her. She hadn't considered lining up her strengths and background with potential career paths that fit. We then worked on giving her the confidence to approach the right hiring managers, connect with them, and try to get some conversations scheduled.

To build that confidence, I helped her deep dive into her background and experience, and then line it up with real jobs that actually exist in today's marketplace. Matching her qualifications with the types of companies that would suit her rekindled her drive. We ended up writing a list of the top ten companies in the area that she could approach.

"Go home and look at these ten companies," I instructed, "and then come back and tell me which ones you're interested in having me connect you to."

The homework I gave this woman is a very important process a person must go through, no matter who they are.

You too will want to figure out all of the companies in your desired geography that you would love to work at. Also take into consideration where you can add the most value. First, try searching for companies where you'll be able to do something that you're already at least semi-good at to create value for the company and inspire their interest since you can give back. Of course you also want to have some personal growth, too.

Next, write a list of the companies you could be valuable to because you are super passionate about them. For instance, if you are raising a child with diabetes or are personally affected, you may want to research companies specializing in diabetes care in the area. Because you know so much about living with the condition and understand the challenges of being a patient, you could add immense value to their organization.

Don't overlook things that happen on the personal front that can apply to the workplace. At times, our own personal mission can become the greatest source of passion from which we can create the highest value.

ACTION ITEMS:

- **Know your definition of success:** Determine what makes you happy in this life—your calling.

- **Turn your passion into a job:** Align what inspires you with your strengths.

- **Clearly define your ideal job:** Record the list of attributes that make a job your ideal job.

- **Seek advice from mentors:** Ask which professions offer the intersection of those attributes.

- **Create a shortlist:** Determine your possible career opportunities.

- **Do your homework:** Interview people working in those professions and get a reality check.

MINDSET

Controlling your mind and reframing your thinking controls your physiology and your outcome. As such, your mindset is the single most important factor that will determine your success in life.

Let me repeat:

Your mindset is the single most important factor that will determine your success in life.

"Anything is possible" should be your mindset. The minute you start thinking something is not possible, it won't be. Reframing your individual thoughts every single time you begin to think negatively is how you retrain your overall mindset. We'll work more on that in the next section, but in the meantime, you need to stop defeatist thinking about yourself and your goals and move past those thoughts because they simply aren't true.

The best way to mitigate limiting beliefs is to always be conscious of what I said at the beginning of this book: it is very likely that everything you aspire to do has already been done. Other people run marathons; you too could run a marathon. Or build a company. Or become a CEO. Of course it will be scary, and inevitably you'll be nervous.

We *all* get nervous when we're operating outside our comfort zone—it's human nature. I get nervous if I'm doing something I've never done before or that I'm largely under-qualified to be doing. But I always try to bring myself back to the thought that everyone living life to the fullest is doing something they haven't done before. Everyone that has ever set a record or reached a milestone had a first time, a beginning. Think of the most successful person you can bring to mind, and use them as inspiration. Even find a way to meet them if possible. In whatever way you can, look to that person's example as a framework to start from. Keep reminding yourself that if someone else has done this already, you can too. If other people can do it—and have done it—you're next. In my executive search business, we see it daily. The CEOs are younger and younger—almost all of them are first-time CEOs. I was a first-time CEO at one point—every CEO was a first-time CEO at some point. And although you might feel nervous when it's your turn, all of the people looking at you realize you're doing it for the first time. And despite you never having done it before, they've chosen you for the role. They believe in you. Now you just have to believe in yourself.

The single best way to control that nervous energy and gain confidence is to monitor your thoughts and practice speaking to yourself in a positive way. Talk to yourself when you're out walking, exercising, or driving to work. I love affirmations and find them extremely helpful. If you were to look around my house, you would see I have little cards everywhere that tell me things I need to remember on a daily basis.

I have one near my sink every morning when I get ready. It says, "Dream bigger than the sky and deeper than the ocean." It's a great reminder to be wide open with my dreaming and to believe in what is possible. (And it's *all* possible.)

Another one I have says, "Don't look back, you're not going that way." In other words, always be looking forward, always be looking for possibilities.

We're *all* students in need of motivational reminders in our lives. If you have to place them on cards around your home, do that. They're really powerful. Put them on your refrigerator or as a rotating screensaver on your computer. Every time one comes up, you see something you need to remember. Keeping yourself motivated is a constant, never-ending ritual you need to practice, practice, practice.

Repetition creates belief.

When you hear something over and over again, you will begin to believe it.

For example, your parents may have taught you that you could do and/or be anything, but do you think your parents actually believed that for themselves? Your parents probably had hard lives and wanted the world for their children; they wanted them to have every aspiration and access to every possibility. I think everything all of our parents did was in an effort to make a better life for us as their children, even if at times that may not have seemed to be the case. I can't speak for all parents, but I know this is certainly how mine operated. How did they keep *themselves* pushing on? What did they tell themselves to help them continue?

In retrospect, I often think about the power of the statements they were probably repeating to themselves on a consistent basis. Their genuine belief in themselves must have created such a positive difference in their lives, but it can also explain their limitations.

My sister interviewed my father with the goal of recording his answers to important questions as he neared the end of his life. She asked him who he admired most in the world. He replied that it was me. It was so heartfelt. I was amazed and humbled that my dad would think that about his middle daughter—of all the people he could have said in the universe.

He was the one who made me believe I could do anything. As such, I went forth into the world growing, getting knocked down, getting up again, and not quitting until I succeeded. It's because of *him* that I became the person he admired most. I'm not sure my father could see the role he played in creating the person he admired most in the world, however. I will never forget my dad's efforts and the challenges he faced with courage in his own right. I consider him the most influential person in my life because of them.

You have the opportunity to create a cycle like this for those around you now and going forward. Just as your parents are often some of the most influential figures in your life, if you have children, you can make a huge difference in how they move in the world just by giving them positive reinforcement over and over again—no matter how old they are. Please start now, and don't stop. And also pay attention to the way you view yourself—it will be transparent to those you mentor and will be included in their perspective as they grow and form opinions in addition to the mindset foundation you're providing.

Although I was programmed to think this way by my parents, I eventually realized that ultimately this was *my* mind and I am controlling it—just as yours is your own too. If your parents didn't support you to think this way, please stop blaming them. What's done is done, but what you choose to do now going forward is all that matters. Regardless of whether you received positive reinforcement in your own life growing up or not, decide right now to take ownership and become your own coach and mentor. You will no longer allow negative self-talk. You are only going to believe in possibilities.

All of this can be learned through repetition. Start now. Do as much reading and as much reflecting as you can. Attend self-improvement seminars—do anything and everything that helps you recognize you are in control of your thoughts and your life. Because you are.

This life is yours. It's not your parents' life, or your partner's, or your kids'—it's *yours*. Take responsibility for it. Bad things may have happened in the past, but they don't have to dictate your future. You are not your circumstances.

Although you can't control what happens to you, the one thing you can always control is who you choose to be in response to what happens to you.

And ultimately that's what will change the trajectory of your life. Choose powerfully. This is your life. It's time to live it your way.

SELF-TALK

When we have a voice in our head that tells us only negatives, it reinforces our limiting beliefs. You'll need to learn to recognize limiting thoughts when they pop up and train yourself to reframe them.

Those types of limiting thoughts aren't allowed in my universe, and they shouldn't be allowed in yours, either. I can't think of a time when I let limiting beliefs control me, simply because I don't allow myself to have them. I've made a really conscious effort to fight against them when they crop up, and it's a conscious daily decision that you too will need to make.

Positive self-talk is critical. Start by replacing all negativity—namely that voice in your head—from continually popping up to repeat refrains of what you don't like about yourself. When I hear that voice, I stop it and instead talk about the characteristics I *do* like about myself.

If that voice were an external person speaking to you, it would be easier to cut them out of your life and never listen to them. You would just walk away and shut them down. That's exactly what you need to do with any negative thought or to the voice in your head—shut it down. Immediately. Have a zero tolerance policy, and learn to control that voice with absolute conviction and authority. Once you've firmly said no and disallowed the negative thought, immediately think about the things about yourself that you value and are really good at or that you really like about yourself.

When negative thoughts come up telling you that something you desire to achieve is impossible, dismiss them with, "It is possible and I *am* going to do it." You need to cultivate a reaffirming voice inside yourself and listen to it.

One of my first executive inspirations was Tony Robbins. I love inspirational speakers; in fact, becoming one was an aspiration at one point in my career. Because of Tony Robbins and his views on mindset, I believe that mind-over-body works every time. In order for that to happen, however, you must believe it is possible and that you're capable. The firewalk is the perfect example of the power of absolute intention combined with positive mindset at work.

Fifteen years ago in San Francisco, I attended a Tony Robbins event. The morning of the event's first day, organizers began empowering the crowd for that evening's firewalk. It started small, with talk of throwing off our self-limiting beliefs. They told us stories of successes and the power of positive, outcome-focused thinking. At the beginning, I had no intention of partaking in the firewalk. Come late evening, we were standing on chairs, literally dancing in anticipation, denouncing everything that held us back, discarding limiting beliefs, and doing everything to elevate the mind-body connection that would empower us to walk on fire.

At 11 p.m., we all stood in front of long lines of hot coals set ablaze. Organizers directed us to firmly plant our feet, square our shoulders, and present our most confident power pose. "Walk purposefully without hesitation," we were told. "Take every step with confidence and focus on your goal. If you're not in the right mindset," we were warned, "your feet will burn."

We were all enthusiastic. The energy and excitement from inside had stayed with us and we were jazzed—we were ready! The parking lot of the Hyatt was filled with executives and CEOs ready to walk across fiery coals. No fear rippled through the crowd. No one seemed hesitant or unsure.

One after another, each business woman and man stepped onto the hot coals and made their way down the burning path. I watched them go and go and go until I finally reached the front of the line. Waiting seemed like the hard part, but now I stood in front of a football-length stretch of flaming coals—and attendants who proceeded to shovel even more burning coals on top.

When I placed my first foot on the coals, I felt the heat in my sole and almost gave into the feeling of fire on flesh. Instead, I immediately reframed my mind, got my metaphorical cool back, and concentrated on the idea I was supposed to focus on: this is *possible*.

And it worked.

By setting aside my limiting beliefs and not giving them one bit of credence in my mind, I walked across the coals purposefully. At the end of my walk, those same attendants threw water on my feet.

When I went home that night, I climbed into bed next to my husband and gently prodded him awake. He rolled over and stared at me with bleary eyes, but I had to share the electricity running through my body with someone.

"Tonight was the most remarkable, amazing thing," I whispered to him. "Mind-over-body actually does work."

The next day, I went in for the second half of the event still reeling from the excitement and empowerment of the previous evening. Inside the lobby, I began chatting with a man I had spoken with the day before. Of course, I wanted to talk about the firewalk.

"How'd the firewalk go for you?"

"Well," he replied. "I have blisters all over my feet."

His experience of the walk took me completely by surprise—a little small hotspot on my foot the next day was my reminder that it actually did happen. When I told him as much, he shrugged.

"I wasn't taking it seriously. Then I stepped on the coals and now my feet are completely burned."

"Oh my God," I thought to myself, "There it is. Right there. It's really true that you have to control your mind, and then your body will not succumb to the hot coals. It actually can be done."

That's why Tony Robbins includes the firewalk in his seminars—it serves as a verifiable, tangible example of the power of positive mindset.

In that first moment, I stepped onto the coals and felt the heat. But I was able to put it out of my mind.

Learning how to control your thoughts to only allow positivity is an exercise that will change your external reality. If you don't believe me, consult other people who have walked across hot coals, completed an IronMan, or who have participated in the Polar Bear Plunge. And then do something like that yourself. Do whatever you need to do to create a powerful and tangible experience of feeling the fear, pushing past it, and conquering your thoughts. Everyone needs to conquer this mindset shift to be successful. Anything is possible and you can do it. Find a way to believe that for yourself. Start cultivating it now.

DARING TO DREAM BIG

"Higher than the sky, deeper than the ocean."

I mentioned this affirmation earlier, but to me it's so much more than a saying on a card: this sentence sums up my worldview. I can't imagine of thinking about the world in any other way.

In life, I believe we are just scratching the surface of what is possible, and I feel the same way about my company. We, too, are only scratching the surface of what we can achieve. Everything we do is ultimately so small in the scheme of things. For me, the only limitations are our physical restraints—the sky and the ocean are the biggest limits.

Those really are my *only* limits. If anyone tries to assign goals for my performance, that's all well and good, but to me those goals are imaginary. I'm going to strive for my highest potential self. It's not a competition with other people—it's competing with myself for what is possible for *me*. Internal drive is essential to actually achieving and succeeding. You'll need to aspire beyond what anyone else expects of you.

If you weren't trained as a "possibility thinker" by your parents, mentors, or people around you, then as I said before, you'll need to read, practice, and study to fill the gaps. You create your self-talk and you control your mind. I've already mentioned a few resources which helped me.

Dreaming big is something totally different than a mere mindset shift. Dreaming big is part two of that skill set. You have to bring yourself to the ground level first: belief. Possibility is next. How do you bridge that chasm?

Start by testing things out—secure smaller successes. Then realize that you're going to keep going so that you never hit a ceiling, since your potential doesn't have an upper limit. As you keep learning and growing, your possibility expands. This means that as you evolve and achieve, as long as you continue to cultivate a growth mindset, you'll never reach the destination of your human potential since the finish line keeps moving and advancing.

And along the way, you'll have to map your dreams out. Literally.

Draw the roadmap from where you are today to your "blue sky" or ideal vision as you can see it now. Maybe you have a gigantic aspiration and the reason it feels so gigantic is that you have no idea how to get there. You may ask, "How in the world can I draw the map because I've never been there before? It's like trying to get to the North Pole, for heaven's sake."

You can dream big and have no exact idea of how to get there. In the wise words of Dr. Martin Luther King, Jr., "You don't need to see the whole staircase. Just take the first step."

In order to draw the career map, you need to go to external resources and meet people at the points along the way to your goal. Those people will help you draw the career map, and each subsequent meeting you have will help you figure out what is between point A and point Z, point by point. There are other people in the world who do know how to help you get there—you just need to find and connect with them. Remembering that everything has been done before is a very, very helpful and optimistic truth.

You may be asking how to start if you don't even know your dream? You start when you realize you're surviving—not thriving—and you start looking ahead to change that. When I was still working in a laboratory, I realized I wanted to be in sales. That's as far as my view would go for about three years. I couldn't get beyond that vision because I wasn't in sales—yet. That was such a Herculean, gigantic vision for me: to have to step out of one field and into another.

Once you take that first step and you decide to make a change, you just need to climb that first mountain. Keep your focus right there. And then as you ascend, and when you hit your first milestone goal—your first victory along the way—take a moment to stop and look around. You'll notice that on the journey your viewpoint changes. The higher you climb, the more perspective you'll gain. And from that new vantage point, the landscape will look different. You'll begin to see other peaks to climb, and figuring out your next move along the path will become easier as you go.

Remember that rain is needed to make things grow, so if and when the storms of your life arrive, you need to embrace them, too. Keep going. Stay positive. Sometimes you have to step through a few chapters of your career before you can see the road to your biggest aspiration.

As you advance, continue to put yourself in situations you wouldn't normally find yourself in, because comfort zones are growth limiting.

Leaving your comfort zone doesn't mean doing something that's far afield from your passion, however. You should always aspire to be in your passion place. And until you're there, you shouldn't be satisfied. You don't have to settle. There are plenty of occupations for which your skills will be graciously applied—best to find one in a place where your passion can intersect with your talent to truly live the life of your dreams.

PREPARATION AND PRACTICE

For anything difficult you have to do in life, combining preparation and practice is the only way to go about it. There are three steps in the process: Preparation, Rehearsal, and Dress Rehearsal.

To begin, you'll need to prepare. For any important meeting, for example, write notes and take them into that meeting.

"Are those notes?" someone may ask you.

"Of course," you should reply. "This is a really important topic and I wanted to be prepared."

Never let someone's possible negative reaction be a deterrent from bringing notes. Why shouldn't you bring notes? It shows you're prepared and really care about getting the facts straight.

Practice is the next step in the process, and it's broken into two stages: Rehearsal and Dress Rehearsal.

In the first stage, it's important to practice hearing how you sound to others around you.

I grew up in sales, where word choice and delivery is of the utmost importance. It was drilled into us to always be conscious of how we speak because the word selection we use and how we say those words affects the tone of what we're saying, and ultimately the response we will receive.

Here's a brief exercise to test it out yourself. Say the following sentences aloud, emphasizing the italicized word each time. Listen to how the connotation changes:

- Peter from *Accounting* shouldn't have left that file on his desk.

- Peter from Accounting *shouldn't* have left that file on his desk.
- Peter from Accounting shouldn't have *left* that file on his desk.
- Peter from Accounting shouldn't have left *that* file on his desk.
- Peter from Accounting shouldn't have left that file on *his* desk.

Small differences in your delivery change the meaning completely. Be thoughtful enough to first prepare, and then practice, practice, practice.

As I mentioned before, talking out loud on a hiking trail, in your car, or in your office is a great avenue to practice.

Another option is to record your calls and listen to how you actually sound. I think any of us who are public speakers find that when we record ourselves we realize that we say "um" a lot more than we thought we did. We're also not always as concise as we want to be. Athletes watch "game tape" religiously, and we—as corporate athletes—need to do the same. It's a really powerful tool for your own growth and advancement.

The next stage of that practice is the Dress Rehearsal. Mentally going through the scenario a few times and imagining the possible outcomes will help you anticipate how you will be received. This is a technique known as visualization. Visualization is important as a mental exercise, but it works best in tandem with—and not as a replacement for—the effectiveness of a practical run-through. You need to get the necessary pitch variation and the muscle memory of your movements down, so make sure you do the initial Rehearsal stage first.

Although it may be my "first time" doing something during a big meeting, I've practiced it at least once through *actual* practice—and then again through visualization (sometimes multiple times).

The difference between showing up unpracticed versus exuding the demeanor of a polished executive is amazing. It's what we call "executive presence" in the search industry. The way you deliver your message(s) is really, really important. And people will remember how you deliver it, often more than they remember precisely what you've said.

After you've crafted what you want to say, your delivery of the message is something you'll still want to keep repeating through visualization and actual practice. Arrive early and sit in a place where you can actually see the person you're meeting, if possible. When they come to retrieve you, make a positive impression by being alert and ready. Pay attention to the posture and physicality you plan to have when you speak with someone (this includes your confident handshake). Voice quality is another important factor. When you're speaking, maintain eye contact and have confidence in your word choices. The combined effect of all of these things works wonders to ensure a powerful first impression.

Putting people at ease quickly is a really good skill to work on as well. When you meet strangers, how can you immediately find a point of connection and get them to a safe place? We're all nervous when we start conversations; you have to find that ability to form a human bond with someone without crossing the line to unprofessional by acting too personal.

The other day, I was with a professional colleague who didn't know of a good way to wrap up and leave her current conversation when she was ready to move on to another person at a networking event. Through that experience I realized that I'm actually quite skilled at that. Here's what I like to say:

"Well, it's been great talking with you." [Insert pause] "I do need to move on, because I have others I need to meet tonight. We should talk again later, though, here's my card."

You just need to make your exit and not be shy about it. Women tend not to be the most skilled networkers, in my experience, because they don't want to be rude. Having a go-to question to begin a conversation and an exit strategy to end one is a good way to approach networking. And practicing helps immensely.

Practice includes all preparation—even thinking about power poses. For example, if you're in the hallway getting ready for a meeting, the single best pose you can do is a "Superwoman" pose. Put both hands on your hips, with your legs wider than shoulder-width apart and your chest out; it's a very powerful pose. And it can immediately take you into a positive, confident mindset. If you are about to have an important call or meeting with someone and want to perform strong, just do that for five seconds before you walk into the room or get on the phone. Two full minutes is ideal, but even five seconds will make a difference. Harvard social psychologist Amy Cuddy presented an entire TED Talk about how power poses and physicality change your experience, entitled *"Your Body Language Shapes Who You Are."*

Part of being aware of your body language is actually remaining present not just in your mind, but also in your body throughout the day. Often, people are living entirely in their heads, disconnected from their bodies—especially when they work in an intellectual environment or are sitting at a desk all day. On a very strong day you feel great and completely present in your body, and this can also work in reverse: if you are present in your body, through power poses and movement you can actually create a very strong day. And once you've fostered this mind-body connection you'll want to maintain it by practicing every day.

For me, it comes back to physicality and movement. Stretching is an incredibly powerful method of enhancing the mind-body connection. For years when I was traveling for business, I learned a forty-five minute yoga series. I still do it in my hotel room between the beds—you don't need a lot of room. Sometimes, I'm in these really tight, small box-like rooms but I can always still find space. Even if you think you don't have physical room for exercise, just throw a towel on the floor and stretch. It makes you feel amazing and everybody can do it. I'm really in favor of things that anyone can do: walking and stretching are great examples. These are two of the best things we can do for ourselves, and yet we seem to always neglect doing them.

So how do we stop neglecting these things? How can we create these habits and achieve the big dreams?

By having intention, discipline, and a possibility mindset.

And how do you create a possibility mindset if that's not native to who you are?

Practice.

Try them all and stick with anything that gets you to the core of yourself. Connect your inner strength to the outer person that you're presenting to the world. This is the connection of mind and body— and it lets you walk across fire.

TOOLS

I've already talked about my experience with Tony Robbins' program, and there are many more excellent personal and professional development programs out there. Their power comes from getting you out of your everyday life and routine and allowing yourself to focus exclusively on your own development and growth over a very intense and specifically designed period of a few days.

You create your self-talk, and you control your mind. If that doesn't come naturally to you, or you weren't taught how to do this properly, now is the time to learn.

There are plenty of amazing books to learn from to acquire the right mindset for success. One such book is *The Untethered Soul* by Michael A. Singer. It supports what we talked about earlier in this chapter: controlling the voice in your head and not allowing it to run wild. We all have the negative inner voice, but you can choose to not listen to it and center yourself, and eventually it does fade into becoming a rare occurrence. If you're struggling to reframe your mindset and really believe you deserve the best for yourself, reading his book will help.

If you're struggling to find your place in an ever-evolving society, there's also an amazing book by Desmond Tutu, Dalai Lama, and Douglas Carlton Abrams called *The Book of Joy* which shares how to find lasting happiness in a changing world. It details what's really important in life and helps you put the power of control back in your hands. It teaches that how you behave every single day will ultimately control your destiny in the end.

My favorite book of all time, however, is *Save the World and Still Be Home for Dinner*. Unfortunately the author, Will Marré, passed away from a surfing accident just weeks after I helped him launch on stage the Institute of Leadership Synergy Program for Women that he developed with National University in San Diego. Will was simply amazing. In his career, he had created the Smart Power Academy (SPA) for women, he trained companies to be "gender friendly," he worked with Stephen Covey's leadership organization, he climbed mountains, and he wrote inspirational books. His dream in creating the new Institute was to empower a million women by leveraging a million men as their mentors.

"We all need to develop Purple Brains," he would say, "because there is a syndrome of Blue Brain thinking that goes on in the executive world today, which we can change, and men are an important part of the solution."

"Blue Brain," as he calls it, refers to male-dominated neuro-network behaviors, and "Pink Brain" refers to these female-dominated neuro-network traits summarized in the list below:

FIGURE 1.0

NEURO-NETWORK Blue Brain	NEURO-NETWORK Pink Brain
• Authoritarian	• Holistic
• Competitive	• Systems
• Reductionist	• Interdependent
• Simple	• Variable
• Linear	• Complex
• Static	• Intuitive
• Sequential	• Anticipatory
• Analytical	• Social
• Facts	• Emotional
• Details	• Versatile

Per Marré, a fully-formed executive exhibits SMART power and has a "Purple Brain"—a combination of the two—since traits from both brains are necessary for successful leadership.

When giving people interviewing and career guidance, I advise women to emphasize their strengths in leadership, employee development, and team-building, while also practicing analytical thinking and concise communication.

The first year I founded my company, I read Marré's *Save the World* book. In it, he talks about the traditional model of working for monetary gain in our careers and then growing. And once we've grown enough, we typically feel it is time to give back.

"Flip it on its head," he once said to me. "Give first, even early in your career when you don't have much. You will gain tremendously from that and then you will grow."

That taught me something important: you don't have to quit your day job to make a difference. For instance, you can support the non-profits you care about while working yourself in your chosen occupation, since it is often quite lucrative. In fact, you can be a lot more powerful if you continue to work in the place where you can generate some income and then share your resources.

That first year after I read Marré's book, I decided every time I made a placement in executive search I was going to create ten jobs in the developing world through microfinance. Essentially, microfinance allows underserved or disadvantaged populations to start businesses. They can take out micro-loans that require much less credit than traditional business loans. Women and scrappy startups are often short on investors and need to finance their own businesses. Microfinance allows them to start their endeavors and to leverage their amazing business acumen to create personal wealth and to support and educate their families. Those are the kinds of "A-ha!" moments that make what I do feel even more meaningful. I love my job and I love what I do, but I'm always asking myself how I can impact more people with it. In this case, microfinance was a really powerful tool I could use to help small companies and—more specifically, women—to create their futures.

When you do this type of giving, you get paid back many times over; not only does it make you feel good, but the business ventures you support make contributions to society.

Being the best human you can be while you're trying to find and pursue your passion is essential because everything converges—you find your passion when you're being the best human you can be.

are dedicated to exceptional performance at work, you need to get in the habit of nurturing the vehicle and its engine that will take you there.

It's a constant, lifelong vigil that is required to keep yourself very physically fit, watch what you eat, and pay attention to what you're burning off. You can't eat junk food and expect to be healthy and high-functioning. We live in the most complex machine imaginable. Respect the boundaries of that machine and give it good fuel for peak performance.

It doesn't matter what your aspiration is, you want to do it in the best physical shape you can manage, because that way:

- It's going to be more enjoyable.
- It's going to be easier to accomplish and achieve.

To me, there's actually no choice when it comes to being physically fit and active; it's part of the success equation.

Depending on the profession you choose, a personal brand that says, "I'm the whole package and I actually look on the outside the way I think and feel on the inside" may well be important to land the job. That is certainly the case for executives.

For better or for worse, people make judgments about your physical fitness and often align that with motivation. They will possibly underestimate you, which could produce negative effects. They will potentially make assumptions about your discipline based on physical appearance.

Personally, I don't like those risks.

Why give anyone any reason to initially doubt you? When your fitness level supports the level of energy required for peak performance in the role you're in, chances are good the exterior lines up, too. Being an executive is a demanding role. Make sure you're in shape for it. Your body—and your mindset—will thank you for it.

DRIVE: YOUR OWN DEFINITION OF "SUCCESS"

For me, the definition of success is happiness. No woman or man can be successful unless they feel happy with their lives as a whole. In my personal experience, it really has nothing to do with money. So what notions of success drive me as an executive woman?

I always want to have room for continued development. If I'm not learning and growing, then I can never be truly happy. I need to always be reaching for something, so—being a growth-minded person—the ability to grow is part of my definition of success. I'm always underqualified for everything I'm reaching for, but I have to have that growth potential. At the same time, I also want to have financial security which to me means I don't want to worry about money. Money isn't the driver—I want to be financially secure so I can just put that aside as something I don't need to worry about.

The most important factor for me would have to be working with amazing people every minute of every day. And I want to handpick them if I can. Over time, I've evolved to the point where I want to choose. If you're able to build a company, you've earned that ability, which is amazing; it's been one of the greatest joys of my life.

I've always wanted to leave the world a better place and I think most people do too. In the beginning of a career, it's often about survival. In the end, it should be about making a difference and really doing something with your talent. You want to find something amazing you can leverage for good. Whether that's having children, a career, building something, making something, launching a company, whatever it is—are you leaving this world a better place? Why are you here? What is your purpose? When you know your purpose, you can go inside yourself and figure out what you're really, really good at and how to help accomplish these goals.

I think everyone is here for a purpose; the next step is figuring out how to leverage that purpose for good. Meaningful work has always been a big driver for most female candidates, probably to a greater extent than for male candidates, in my experience. Millennials are also really centered on this. At the core of everyone's being, we want to have meaningful work. But we also want to be learning and growing.

I often tell employers, "If you want to make your company *really* attractive, make it attractive to women and Millennials who both want the same thing: meaningful work and the ability to grow in their careers."

Now, let's talk about the financial security piece. If it's not about money as the end goal, how much would make you feel free enough to make choices in life? The minute you have enough money, you have options. According to *The Atlantic*, Betsey Stevenson and Justin Wolfers refined a thesis Wolfers began working on in the '70s to say that "well-being continues to increase with more money, but at a rate proportionate to your income." When you're a successful career woman, you're going to reach that point. Then, the excess money won't matter at all. I know from experience that when you get into your sweet spot where you're doing what you love, it doesn't feel like work. And the money feels unlimited because it becomes so much easier to generate value. You're lining yourself up with a job that gives you way more than merely monetary revenue.

Maybe you choose to volunteer because it gives you incredible emotional satisfaction (it enriches you in a different way), but you do need your minimum needs covered. There's a formula for your minimum needs plus a safety cushion for emergencies, and then, beyond that, it's all extra. Put it in the bank for future security. If you are achieving more than your number now, you're building for retirement. That's a nice vision, but I really think that focusing on that too early in your career can really hold you back. If you believe in a much more proportional and greater return, once you find it, you'll stop looking.

Another benchmark of success for me is being listened to and having my ideas seriously entertained. Hopefully, one of them will be the one to make a positive change for an organization. Without the ability to be heard, we become rapidly discouraged and conflicted—which results in burnout. We need to be supported by people around us that intend to help us grow as a person, not just as an employee.

My version of success is also feeling comfortable that I am enough, and that what I've achieved is not about trying to impress others. I think we're programmed to worry about what other people think at a very young age. Learning how to put that aside and just worry about what you think and feel can be a battle, but it's one worth fighting. Recognizing what success means to you will reveal your own drivers and motivators, eliminating the need to be concerned with other people's benchmarks of success.

'Am I growing as a person and making a difference or giving back? Am I feeling financially sound?' Ask yourself these questions and shut down the voice in your head that might be saying, "What about the Joneses?" It really has no bearing on whether or not you can settle in and be happy. Once you quiet that voice, you will feel absolutely confident that nobody can rock your universe with something you may have wished you had done or possessed. You won't be trying to impress anyone else or living your life to meet anyone else's expectations. Life is too short to put the key to your happiness in someone else's pocket. Know your own version of success and go after it.

As you grow up, measuring yourself by standards other than your own becomes less and less important. "Wow," you'll say. "I wasted so much time thinking about what other people thought." So how can you fast track letting go of what people think before that becomes the case? The best way is to sit down with mentors who actually have become very accomplished and ask them about it. "Was there a switch in your mindset at some point that helped to get you to stop worrying about what other people thought about you, and if so, how can I flip it in my own mind?"

Look at examples of other people who only followed their own ideas of success. Again, I'm a firm believer that everything you want to do has already been done. If the people you deem to be successful are telling you that it really doesn't matter what other people think, and you have absolute confidence in their word, it's going to be easier to create the same belief within yourself.

If validation is the number one shift, the number two shift is confidence—the confidence to say, "I am my own person and I don't have to live by anybody else's rules." Don't compare yourself to others. The unfortunate reality of social media and the reason people stay on it as much as they do is that we use it to make judgments. We compare ourselves to others the entire time and that is a really unhealthy behavior. Everybody has a unique gift and core values they believe in. I would encourage you to look internally to those beliefs instead of externally at other people's. Many people who live their lives for other people don't have enough confidence and belief in themselves to recognize their unique gifts and purpose.

Develop your confidence in whatever way possible: it could be through coaches, counselors, or books. I'm a huge reader of self-development books, not just on the business side but on the personal side as well. There's so much that you can learn; we make life so complicated for ourselves and it doesn't have to be. It's as simplistic as living your life for you, realizing you are unique, and not caring what anyone else thinks about it. Do your best in this world, make your best impression, and leave the world a better place.

It's hard to be self-realized when you're five years old, and yet even as we grow older we develop bad habits that exacerbate the problem and hold us back from living our best life because we're missing this key ingredient. As a parent, I would ask that you give your children that confidence. Tell them, "You can do and be anything you want. The world is your oyster. Make *your own* choices. I will support you no matter what. No matter who you are."

This can be a really hard thing for a lot of parents, just letting their children be who they are and really embracing and empowering who they're meant to be. They're little genetically-unique selves. Please do not place your own personal expectations on them for who they should become, because then they'll grow up trying to live their lives for other people.

Look at yourself—you may be trying to undo a lot of what was instilled in you before you had any awareness that it was happening. The fact that you're reading this book means you have awareness and hope to move beyond that. If you're a parent, don't make your children bend to your ideals and expectations. Let them develop their own.

Reminders all over your house that say things like "You're unique" would be awesome to help your family AND yourself through the use of positive affirmations. If you're really struggling with this concept of uniqueness and being your own person, then surround yourself with reminders and people who practice it. Wherever you are along your trajectory, embrace your uniqueness and just be yourself. And for any woman in her forties or fifties who might be even slightly concerned about aging, I want to assure you that it just gets better and better as you go. I'm over fifty and I have become so much more confident with every year that passes. In the end, all of the ridiculousness of living your life by other people's standards starts to melt away as long as you keep developing yourself to your fullest capacity. You came with certain gifts and, whatever those gifts are, you'll be well served to amplify and apply them via a career you love and one you are naturally good at.

It's not just your career that should enhance you; there's value in your immediate community. Choose people to be around who are different and really embrace their idiosyncrasies—it will liberate and empower you to do the same. When you hang out with people who espouse those values and have confidence, all of those good things will rub off on you. Anybody who makes you feel smaller than you are will hold you back in life. Eliminate those toxic relationships; if you have to make yourself smaller to be around them, they're not your people. You have the ability to be whatever you want and the company you keep should embrace that mindset.

ACTION ITEMS:

- **Gauge your Mindset:** Determine what you need to do to shift your mindset to a positive one.
- **Change your Self-Talk:** Tailor how you talk to yourself to increase positivity; train yourself to reframe negative thoughts.
- **Identify a "stretch challenge":** Commit to do it (skydiving, marathon, etc.) and choose a deadline.
- **Create a mindset action plan:** Outline specific resources and action items.
- **Schedule Self-Care time:** Include time for thinking and exercising.
- **Define Success:** Create your own detailed definition of success, including specific ingredients that are important to you personally.

COACHES
AND MENTORS

Identifying people to be your mentors is an important step. You need to speak to career coaches and other advisors to talk through plans and get perspective. Having career coaches throughout your entire executive life will help at different stages of your journey. Look for those doing what you want to do, but don't limit yourself based on any demographic.

More than half of my early mentors were male, because those were the people in positions of authority at the time at my prior companies. However, I believe it is important that mentors be both male and female. Why? First off, there aren't enough experienced female mentors to go around, particularly given the majority of industries can be male dominated. And second, even if there were, male mentors present an entirely different—and equally valuable—perspective and point of view as their female counterparts. If you limit yourself to only talking to women, you're missing out on a huge opportunity to learn and grow in a number of different ways.

I recommend you start with mentors in the beginning and move toward specialized coaches as you progress throughout your career. Some people think of coaching as a person telling you what or who to be; I think of a coach as the person that tells you how to be a rockstar. They hone in on what you need to improve and take you to the next level, just as those engaged by top athletes to improve their performance.

You're going to have different specialized coaches at different stages—I've personally had four or five already—and as such, a career coach will be important over the course of your working life. They can be hired one-on-one as an independent consultant, or sometimes they are included as a value-add service in different personal and professional development programs. I joined Vistage, for example, which is a national executive development organization for CEOs. Membership comes with both small group moderated sessions monthly, plus an experienced executive coach who meets with you one-on-one once a month for a few hours. In addition to that, I've hired multiple coaches on the side to focus on different things, ie. specific organizational development and/or strategic planning assistance. A smart entrepreneur will always have a coach to give guidance and to tell them the truth about their leadership style—and how to improve upon it.

Coaches come up with great ideas that you wouldn't necessarily think of which can really enhance your career. Once, I was struggling with how—as the CEO of the company—I could keep alive an amazing culture to motivate and support my employees amongst the myriad of day-to-day responsibilities involved in building a professional services organization.

When posing the challenge to my coach, he turned to me and said, "Create a Culture Committee. Identify the four or five people at your company who embody your culture the best—they can be the committee and the keeper of the mission, vision, and values. They will make sure that this energy lives on."

Building a Culture Committee was a remarkably easy solution that I wouldn't have considered. It has worked like a charm while engaging the employees' minds and hearts. Coaches give you an outside perspective when you may be a little too close to an issue or too overworked to evaluate the situation accurately. Many executive leaders struggle with owning too much and not delegating enough. Coaches can help reinforce the need to delegate and trust. They look at your trajectory and leadership challenges, and then provide ideas from an aerial view, which will make a difference.

MY EARLY MENTORS

You may not have thought of them as mentors, but the people who affected and influenced you early on in life set you up to believe certain things and operate in certain ways. Some mentors are inherently within your home or family and others are people you admired from afar. I'll give you some examples of my own.

One of my first mentors was my father. In the latter part of his career, he became a global executive at General Motors. I was very impressed by that as a child. His career certainly didn't start at the top. At first, he worked the graveyard shift in the automotive factory line, leaving the house before midnight and not returning until I got up to go to school the next morning. That was tragic for me, seeing someone I loved stay awake all night and work on an automotive factory line. But later, his company recognized him for his efforts and he was promoted to a position that took him overseas. He traveled incessantly to remote countries. I thought his international job was the coolest thing, and something I wanted for myself one day. His career progression reinforced for me that anything you want to achieve is truly possible through hard work and determination.

Meanwhile, his much younger brother (he was probably only five years older than me) used to babysit for us when we were kids. My uncle was always an entrepreneurial sort of guy. When he was very young, he bought a marina on Lake Michigan. I used to go out and pump gas and teach people how to water ski with him. He was my hero, both as an athlete and as an executive. Today, he's transitioned from CEO to retirement after having enjoyed the success of building multiple businesses over the course of his career. Success started early for him because he was so confident and positive. He taught me to believe in myself at an early age. He encouraged me to learn how to trick ski backwards and to water ski off ramps because he believed in my potential and the power of positive thinking.

In a totally different way, a very academic aunt of mine left an equally important imprint on my life. When I was young, she became a dentist and moved to Alaska. She didn't enjoy young children, and never had any kids of her own. From her, I learned it's okay to be an executive professional and a woman without children. She was the only woman of her generation I knew with that perspective.

As a sixteen-year-old impressionable teenage girl I went on a road trip vacation with her and my uncle to Florida. I still remember her practicing her lectures out loud to herself as she drove us through the night while my uncle slept. She ultimately went on to become the Dean of the University of Michigan Radiology School, and spoke internationally at academic conferences where her expertise was very much in demand. Watching a career professional woman be so strong, empowered, and in control of her universe was definitely an early mentorship opportunity for me and a lesson in commitment to excellence. Years later, I found the courage to raise my hand and the confidence to use my voice because of the example she set.

My transition to sales wasn't traditional. I actually walked into a competitor company and asked to see the VP of Sales since my current employer didn't believe that laboratory technologists could transition to sales. I touched on this story earlier in this book, but that head of sales not only changed my life by taking a chance on me, but today still remains a great friend of mine. He recognized me as a high potential person and taught me a very simple formula: people need to have three reasons to do something or they won't make a change. That became my mantra. And he still claims today I was his favorite student because whatever he would tell me, I would do. *Wouldn't everyone do that?* I thought to myself. *I mean, it's taking advice from someone who's really successful. Why wouldn't everyone listen?* We still laugh about when he took a chance on me when I worked for him thirty years ago and how he created my sales career. And we shake our heads at, surprisingly, how often people don't listen to someone who knows better.

Later, I worked at a global pharmaceutical company in commercial operations. The man who hired me there was probably the most charismatic, influential guy I've ever known. He went on to be the CEO for multiple companies, and his employees would follow him anywhere given the loyalty he inspired. The guy was just magical in his enthusiasm and engagement. I was in charge of virology and was one of five people hired to build his team. One day he called me into his office.

"I wanted to let you know first that I'm resigning, Robin," he said. "I have this great CEO opportunity that I'm leaving for, but I figured it all out, and you will be my successor. I've already proposed it to leadership—you are taking my job."

I was floored and amazed. On one hand, I was disappointed that he had to leave and we couldn't work together any longer. On the other, it had only been a year or two, and yet he was betting on me! I had earned it, and I was going to become Senior Vice President of a multinational global organization. It just goes to show that if you create value right from the start, someone will look out for you on their way out the door. That same CEO worked with me again later as a trusted, valued client and then again as a CEO candidate before purchasing a winery. We are still great friends, and we remain in touch today.

I've been intentional in maintaining these valuable relationships with my work mentors, and as a result, they have stood the test of time.

People are in your life for a purpose. When I went into executive search, I didn't immediately start my own company; I actually worked for someone else for a brief amount of time who was very seasoned. I was partially through cancer treatment and on chemotherapy, with an IV line in my neck and a fanny pack of drugs around my waist. Fairly immediately, I realized that one day I would need to start my own company so I could do it my way, but in the meantime I worked for him for a few years before leaving amicably to form my own competitor firm. I kept in touch and later acquired that practice and the amazing team I had previously managed. By that time, the former CEO was in his late sixties, and we reversed roles with him coming to work for me in the end.

It was this perfect full-circle progression; we still love each other today, and I'm so happy to have him in my life. Now, he's paddling canoes across a lake in Atlanta and still consulting for the executive search industry while writing his own book. When I resigned from that company to form a competitive firm, it could have been very challenging; given our relationship based upon trust, however, he just let me go. We divided the client list instead of arguing, and were completely honest when clients had a different idea in mind and preferred one of us to the other as their partner. I think it's really, really important that you honor and value the mentorship someone has given you. I will never forget the people who gave me opportunities and took a chance on me; they all believed in me and wanted me to succeed. It's a truly collaborative, cooperative relationship that you develop with whomever is your mentor—particularly if you create value in return for them and make them proud to have bet on you.

MY COACHES

Throughout my career, I had intermittent exposure to coaches; usually, it was something the corporation I was working for provided. Pretty quickly, when I founded my company, I realized CEOs don't have a safe place or a lot of people to talk with. No matter how much you value your employees, you can't discuss strategies with them like: "How am I going to exit this business one day? How am I going to grow if it means changing my job?"

During a group dinner one night, a woman said to me, "Hey, I think you're a biotech recruiter."

"Yes, I am," I replied. "What do you do?"

She was a Chair at Vistage, the organizational development company I described earlier, which specializes in supporting CEOs throughout the U.S. According to Vistage's website, they have over 23,000 members spread worldwide and organized into small groups by location. In my Vistage group, I was the least experienced person—I had one year of being a CEO under my belt and even though we were growing quickly at the time, we had annual revenues of less than $1 million. There were people in our group who had eighteen to twenty-five years of working as a CEO in their industries, and they had stayed in this group the entire time.

At the beginning, I thought to myself, *How can I get any value from this CEO group when it's cross-functional, and members are from all different industries? How can this apply to me? I'm only concerned with life sciences and recruiting. I mean, I don't really care about other businesses like real estate or banking. This is going to be strange.*

But I decided to go out on a limb and learn what I could from an experienced group of cross-functional CEOs in a trusted, valued partner setting. Turns out, all CEOs share very similar problems, and the primary differences lie in the stage of the company you're involved with, versus what industry you're in. Additionally, our group members had a passion for mentoring new CEOs. They became a very large and powerful mentor network that was truly involved in all of San Diego's business dealings... great friends to have.

Early on in my Vistage group, a CEO told me, "You're probably in the happiest stage of running your company: you have a really small group of people working for you and the growth you are experiencing is really exciting. You have a million dollars in revenue, a few key employees running things with you, you're a 'hands on' operator, and you're going to look back on this and think how fun it was." Realizing he was ahead of me on the same journey, I immediately tried to slow down and enjoy the moments with my young team rather than racing through that stage of the company, and I'm happy I did. Retrospectively, he was right and his sage advice was definitely on-target.

We would present our business challenges to other CEOs for their feedback and vice versa. Then, we'd solve business challenges around the table. About five years ago, I left my group, but all of those people are still in my network. My mentor, financial service professionals, legal advisors and non-profit board associations all started at Vistage.

Individually, they each taught me things I never would have learned on my own. Get out of your box enough to know there are people who can help you solve problems. And that your mentors don't necessarily need to be from your industry. Sometimes it's actually better when they aren't, because they're more objective. They may not understand your business, but they understand a lot of different businesses and can point out when something doesn't make sense.

For example, I'm what is known as a "service provider." We sell executive search services to our clients, like a law or financial services firm would, so we're familiar with those models and those firms are familiar with ours. One of the most relevant peer mentors in my group ran a big financial services firm; he had all of the exact same problems I had. He was a brilliant resource to me personally over many years, even when we each left the group.

When I left Vistage, I hired a professional coaching agency to learn more about myself as a CEO and leader. My goal was to talk with my new coach about my business on an even deeper level. It's important to figure out what you're trying to learn from a coach before you hire someone. In this case, I didn't evaluate the coach properly for what I wanted to accomplish. This particular coach focused on CEO development—they coached lots and lots of CEOs, with a focus on enhancing organizational efficiency through improved execution. What I ended up realizing is that what I *really* wanted was a strategy coach. I'm really good at knocking off tasks; I can write a laundry list every day and get them all done. My coach just kept coming up with tons and tons of tactical ideas with me, when what I really needed was someone to think strategically about where I was headed three to five years into the future and to ensure my team was excited about the journey. My greatest question became, "How am I going to achieve the growth I envision, to get from where I am now to where I want to be in the future?"

I have learned while working in executive search that most executive coaches are highly specialized. Armed with this knowledge, the next coach I hired for myself was a woman whose company dealt with CEOs to develop corporate strategy. Defining what you're trying to learn from your coach is critical. And the right coach makes all the difference; there is no way that anyone can do all of this by themselves.

FINDING YOUR COACHES

I suggest you start with free coaches in the beginning—people from your family or work environment who could act as mentors. Hopefully, your bosses are good mentors. Ask employers what kind of mentor or coach they are able to provide before you agree to work for them—will it be your manager, or another assigned resource? Is it a formal mentoring program, or informal and simply a buddy system upon hire? Later in your career, plan carefully, interview and choose a personal coach that meets your needs, regardless of whether your employer will hire one for you or not. People rely too heavily on their employer or company to set them up with or assign them a coach. Coaches are worthy investments; they focus on an individual's specific problems, and a generic company coach often won't tailor their services to you in the same way. A good coach will ask you the really hard questions about yourself. It can be uncomfortable answering questions you haven't had the courage to ask yourself, but it's necessary work to see your career grow.

As if you were seeing a "career therapist," commit to the process and do the work in between sessions, dive deep into self-reflection, and make an effort to better understand yourself. Before you hire your coach, be ready to work on yourself because there will always be room for improvement—you're not as fully formed an executive as you think you are. No matter how good you are, entire organizations dedicated to coaching CEOs exist for a reason. We're all trying to "sharpen the saw" and get better. There are no perfect leaders, and we all have day-to-day challenges. Sometimes things happen that we don't know how to control. Coaches see hundreds and thousands of people from different industries and have an interdisciplinary approach and a large toolkit as a result of their experience coupled with their training. They can effectively solve more problems than one person with one perspective who is too close to the campfire.

So what is important to look for in a coach? It's really important to have good chemistry, that you like and trust this person. If you don't, you're not going to tell them how you really feel. Again, think of it like a therapist: if this person is annoying and doesn't understand you, they're not your person. You may have to try out a few coaches before you find the right fit. Interview more than one and get someone who you think understands you and your issues. They don't have to be your best friend, but you need someone who you respect and will feel accountable to when they ask you to do something hard.

After determining what kind of coaching he or she excels at, find out their track record of success with people like you or companies in your stage and situation. Develop a good vetting process, which includes requesting references and asking for some actual case study examples to show they can do what it is that you'd like them to do. Have a clear vision of what you're trying to accomplish with your coach and be able to spell it out with them. The best coaches will give you a questionnaire or interview you in elaborate detail at the beginning of the assignment—they want to learn about you quickly so that they can be immediately effective. Plus, someone that has you do an exercise full of pivotal questions coupled with a sit-down discussion of your answers is invaluable.

If you choose the wrong person you can waste time, money, and energy—and it can be hard to discontinue these types of contracts. Make sure you don't sign your life away, and ensure you have an easy exit clause. At any moment, you might decide you don't have time or they're not providing value. So be careful about signing up for too much. The best and most expensive coaching program I ever hired had no contract: you had a partnership as long as they were "giving value to you." It was a significant investment at several thousand dollars per month, but the potential for return on investment was quite valuable. It was worth it to me to not have to worry about figuring a way out of a contract. And I liked that they were confident enough to offer services without one. Interestingly, this company wasn't the right fit, and I later selected a less pricey option that suited my needs better. Most importantly, I had to experiment to learn what I really needed.

For a less expensive, starter option for executive women there's an online coaching group called CSweetener that was started by a venture woman in San Francisco. It's amazing. You can sign up for several hundred dollars a year and receive a certain number of coaching sessions. You get to experiment with multiple different coaches with different specializations and personalities. It's a good option to consider, depending upon your needs.

Once you find a coach, how often should you meet with her or him? Seeing your coach every other week is the minimum I would recommend; set aside thinking time for yourself, but don't overdo it. There are all different levels and all different costs of coaches, but if you're running a company and a certain coach will deliver amazing value to this company, don't be afraid to invest more—it'll be a drop in the bucket relative to the potential rewards. This is all about a mindset of investing in yourself. What are you worth and what is this company that you hope to create worth? If you don't have a lot of resources right now, it's really hard to spend money when it hasn't delivered anything yet. I am always a champion of investing and reinvesting, but that's my own personal risk profile. Essentially,

I make a bet on something and invest in it every single day. It can be scary, and coaching might feel like a gamble to some people. But to me it's a safer bet than the alternative: betting on knowledge you don't have.

In my opinion, finding a career coach for candidates is a harder process. If you get laid off by your employer, there are outplacement organizations you may be assigned to if your employer is sizable or is doing a sizable layoff. A great example is the outplacement firm Lee Hecht Harrison. They coach candidates who've been laid off and help them land their next role through resume development, practicing interview and application questions, and coaching them how to answer them effectively.

However, to the best of my knowledge, if your company isn't sponsoring you then you can't leverage their services. For instance, in San Diego we have the Leadership Edge that coaches executives and leadership teams, but they are also typically contracted by the company. There aren't a lot of people who offer this service for individuals. Some independents will claim candidate coaching, but you want to be careful and once again do your research on who you're hiring and their capabilities. Look for a professional coaching credential from a legitimate professional coaching organization.

Executive search firms like mine spend a lot of time coaching candidates we are evaluating for our searches every single day, all day long and typically don't charge for it. I would advocate you focus on boutique, highly specialized search firms in your area of expertise because they will know your industry and they're a free resource if you can get the search professionals to talk to you. Not all search professionals will do this, but my company makes a point to spend time with life science experienced candidates in their moments of need, since we hope to create a strong impression with those people who will become our future customers. And you should in fact seek out executive search professionals specialized in your discipline. They're an essential part of your network and control much of the hiring that goes on from the Director level through VP and CEO roles, so make every effort to try to get to know them and befriend them. They can help you with your career. If a particular search firm is specialized in your vertical, that's the one you want to get to know.

For most search professionals, contact information is readily available on their website or through LinkedIn. It's ideal if you are referred to them by another impressive executive in their network. Please be aware, however, that most search professionals spend the majority of their day seeking to fill their specific assignments and don't always have time to slow down and talk to random candidates. It's a core value of my company to spend time with all impressive unemployed candidates and particularly diversity candidates including women. There are other companies like us if you look hard enough. Random and unexpected encounters are our future, especially if they're women, since they are in high demand in most industries. Search firms that specialize in and value diversity are more inclined to help. Use your resources to find these people. You can meet them at a networking event or figure out where they're speaking. Find a way to meet them. Invite them to have coffee and make it your treat. Do something meaningful for them.

Any professional outfit should slow down and spend at least some time with you. The less senior you are in an organization, the harder it may be because an organization may be focused on completing Director, VP, CEO and Board searches. My business is like this—we don't get involved with junior roles requiring "straight out of college" search. Like executive coaches, each search firm will have a specialization and you have to check what a given organization's is. If they say they're conducting executive search but don't give specifics, ask: "What is the normal stage of career that you are placing, and into which type of companies? Entry level through Director and Vice President? Director through CEO and Board? If they're not playing at your level, they're not going to be able to help you.

At my company, we believe there's a real opportunity for people who coach candidates who are un-sponsored by businesses. A woman who worked for me has moved on to become a candidate coach, and I wish her all the luck in the world because I think there's an unlimited pool of people who need coaching and someone who needs to help them. And to be really valuable to those people, you have to be specialized in that career stage. Everything I talk about in this book is part of a core formula to advance your career, but spending time on a consistent basis with someone who understands your career level is imperative.

FINDING YOUR MENTORS

Knowledge helps you form your voice and gives you confidence. Align yourself with experts in the field you're pursuing with the goal of absorbing their expertise like a sponge. Learn everything you can about trends in that particular area and, through that process, you will continue to evolve your thinking and the thinking in your field. In order to do that, you have to first intimately understand the landscape in which you're operating. Don't be afraid to learn from the leaders in your industry. Bring your burning desire to succeed, cultivate a positive voice of confidence, and choose a successful person to learn from as your inspiration.

A mentor is someone who has done what you want to do and can be one or ten levels beyond you in their career development. What is important is that they're on the path you want to follow and are the professional you want and expect to become. A mentor knows the formula of getting there because they've actually done it—successfully—themselves. Those people are like gold in your career. You have to be looking around you at all times, thinking, "Is this someone who I respect that's actually achieved the career of my dreams? And are they willing to help me?" It doesn't always have to be exactly the thing that you want to do, but it should be at least on a similar path.

And I wouldn't just have one mentor. I would try to write a list of the five to ten people I admire most—a mix of women and men. I really can't emphasize that enough. If you remember my stories, half of them were women, and half of them were men. It's more likely, at present, that your professional mentors will be mostly men in the beginning because historically they've been in executive-level roles for a longer period of time. If you hold out for a female executive, you may delay your progress. Write your list, and if you don't know some of them personally, get a warm introduction from a person they know who has value to them. Approaching a potential mentor "cold" is so much harder than leveraging a warm introduction.

Hopefully there's some point of connection between you two; a warm introduction is what will most often get results. And if there's not, you can still try. I wouldn't discourage you from trying, but if someone I value and trust says I need to meet a person, everything comes to a halt. I stop, I spend the time, and I meet that person.

Having a connection works when you're picking out the company you'd like to work for, meeting a mentor—for many things. Find out who you know that works there, or who knows someone that worked there, or is friends with a person you need to meet. Connections move mountains, and relationships make the world go around.

Once you have a connection, then it's about creativity and really standing out—without doing silly, unprofessional things. For example, when someone sends me an email saying, "'Let's meet at three p.m.!" in the subject line and I've never met this person before, it's unlikely they'll make the cut. Surprisingly I've received many messages like that lately, so it's not even novel or unique anymore. Email typically doesn't work very well these days, either—you need to find a more unique point of entry. If there's someone I admire on the speaking circuit, there are ways to "follow" people where you get notifications when they're doing an event in your area by setting up Google alerts. Then, as a wise and successful friend of mine says: "Get up, suit up, and show up!"

As you start becoming relevant in your industry with the work you do, start attending different people's events and make a point to have a conversation with them about what they just did and said. After they're done speaking and come off the stage, wait in line, hand them your business card, introduce yourself, and shake their hand. Each time, it'll be warmer. People are impressed if you're genuinely a fan of theirs and you put out the effort to learn more about them. Don't be a stalker—but if you're following their career, really follow their career and get involved. If you care about them, they will care about you.

LinkedIn is an incredible resource for career research to help you determine connections you already have who are connected to potential mentors you want to meet. Even though you can see who knows someone at a specific company via LinkedIn, I wouldn't recommend messaging them through the platform as it's very inappropriate and impersonal. Because I have over ten thousand LinkedIn followers, I could not possibly answer all of those messages. Every interaction on the site gets diluted because there's too much noise and too many random people hitting me up for business. You don't want to get caught up in the noise, so I suggest you simply use LinkedIn for research, not for initial contact.

After seeing who knows the person you want to connect with, call those people and kindly ask for their help, since it is very important to you.

"Hey, I'm dying to meet [name of person]. How do you know them? I think we could provide value to each other and I'd like to discuss with them how that could work. Do you know them well, and if so—would you be willing to introduce me?"

Take action. In this case, the actions would be meeting the person, shaking their hand, looking them in the eye and saying, "I've been following your career and admire you so much. The work you do is very impressive and I believe knowing one another could be valuable to us both." Remember that more seasoned people can also choose younger mentors who will help them see themselves as others do over time.

When you've established trust and mutual interest and you're ready to more formally move into the mentor/protege relationship, you can use language similar to this: "I am at the stage of my professional career where I really need some help. I'm hopeful that just by spending fifteen minutes together, I could learn a little bit of your wisdom. I respect and appreciate you as a leader."

Afterwards, follow up with a note letting them know how wonderful it was to meet them. You're not expecting anything in return, just putting yourself on their radar. It works on every level in all industries. And who wouldn't want to help an excited person who admires their career path—especially when they've clearly done their homework?

With coaches, you want to meet with them every other week at a very minimum, but mentors are a bit different. Ideally, you'd meet once a week, but you have to let your mentor set the pace—you don't want to scare them away. How much time do they actually have to spend with you? In some instances, a coffee once a quarter may be all they have time for. In other instances, it could be meeting once a week for coffee.

Giving a standard range of time for a mentor and mentee meeting is hard to do because it's hard to predict how busy a particular mentor will be. And you will need to be respectful of their time because they've agreed to help and support you for free. Don't make it so hard that it's scary or difficult for them, and don't take advantage of their generosity. Sometimes they won't even have any formal meetings with you, just coffee or lunch. Essentially, the goal is to evolve to an implicit relationship where you can call them any time you need help and support.

Several years ago, I received an important award from the San Diego Business Journal, and unbeknownst to me, a young woman in the audience considered me a potential mentor in the field of recruiting. She'd only been in the field for one year, but was very committed to excellence both personally and professionally. She sent me a very kind note thereafter, and asked if she could come by my office for coffee at my convenience. I didn't know her, but I admired her courage, so I said yes. She presented very well in person—she was poised, polished, and professional beyond her years of experience. I knew immediately she'd be a great fit for my organization, and told her as much by the time our meeting was over—even though I wasn't hiring at the time. We promised to keep in close touch, and I would be her mentor. Fast forward about six months and we had the resignation of one of my experienced recruiters, so I thought about her and called immediately. Although she didn't have much experience, she had commitment and huge career development potential. She came in, interviewed well with the team, and landed a new role with my company. I loved the fact that she was so serious about professional development, and it shines through in her work today. That young woman is going places, and I'm proud to work with her daily. We have become close personal and professional friends along the way, sharing a passion for giving back and making a difference in the world.

When it comes to scheduling, let the mentor suggest what works for him or her. Suggesting online meetings and/or video conferences instead of in-person meetings may also help your chances for success. Video has become such a comfortable place for so many people, and it saves time. If you're being thoughtful enough to suggest, "Hey, why don't we just hit a link once a week, I'll set up a recurring meeting," they'll be more inclined to keep the rapport going and speak with you periodically. When you do meet in-person, pay for the lunch or the coffee, and hold the meeting where it's convenient for them. Remember—they're spending their time to meet with you, and a person's time is their most important and valuable asset. It's not a forty-hour work week for most of these people: it's an eighty- to one hundred-hour work week, and now they're donating some of that precious time to you.

If you think about successful CEO-level people, most are earning thousands of dollars per hour and they have agreed to pause their other responsibilities when they sit down with you. Meeting with you is a donation of their time, from the goodness of their heart. Hopefully they're the type of person who really wants to help lead and inspire you. If you haven't read the book *The Go-Giver* by Bob Burg and John David Mann, please check it out. It's important for the protege to have awareness and think about ways to provide some value back to the mentor.

How can this be valuable for them? Can they develop their teaching skills, later introduce you to people they value, claim a stake in your future success, and/or state that they were a mentor of yours once you're successful? Is it important to them to be advancing other women for their career development, too? Is there something in it for them? Bring them a little thoughtful gift or card each time you meet—it's fascinating how far a very small token of appreciation can go. After I did a favor for someone, they brought me a personalized, small gift, which believe it or not is very differentiating. They didn't have to do that and it wasn't expected on any level, yet I so appreciated that they took the time to show gratitude for the value I provided. Those sorts of things may seem trivial, but they can make all the difference. Value their gift of time; their time could be spent doing so many other things instead.

MY FIRST EXECUTIVE MENTOR

At one point, a company I worked for merged with a company in North Carolina and I went there on business. They wanted me to teach everyone there how to sell. On site, there was a female General Manager and CEO who has since gone on to become the CEO of a biotech company and is also now a client of mine. But back then, I worked for her for three amazing years of her 20+ year career with the company. She had joined the company straight out of medical school and started running the North Carolina site. When I arrived I was a young, brazen sales gal acquired through a recent merger, who raised her hand and promoted herself to the newly created opportunity. We struck this unique partnership because she was really good at a lot of things I didn't know how to do yet, and I was really good at selling the company's products and interfacing with customers on every level.

Dressed beautifully, she was very professional and wildly successful—a powerhouse in every meeting—and locally influential in the beautiful town of Chapel Hill. When I later resigned after being recruited to a biotech company in San Francisco, she was quite disappointed because I had been exposed to that company in the context of our working relationship. Resigning was particularly difficult for me, because we had an exceptionally strong friendship and a mentoring relationship. But it was in my best interest both personally and professionally at the time, and I hoped she would eventually understand.

I was very careful and detailed in my communication to preserve the relationship, but corporations can be quite cold in their response. Because the biotech company I was leaving for was considered a competitor, upon resignation, it was company policy that they had to escort me out of the building immediately. I remember walking out with my box of personal belongings. My mentor tried to be as cool about it as she could, but she was sincerely disappointed with me on multiple levels. It was very painful for me to experience, and I wasn't sure if we would ever have a reconciliation.

But the ending to this story is ultimately not a sad one. Not too many years later, we reunited and now I spend valued time with her whenever she's in town. She is a huge fan of my work, and when I'm in North Carolina, I stay at her house. She didn't let a professional decision that was ultimately in my best personal interest stand in the way of our friendship. She's still working as a CEO in my network today, and has also become a trusted, valued customer of my executive search firm. Early in building my company we jointly organized a CEO group trip to Napa for female biotech CEOs—it was a very memorable experience in both collaboration and the power of female friendships in building companies.

FROM EXECUTIVE MENTORS TO EXECUTIVE PEERS

Many female-led companies that share the same customers are cooperative with mine, and I consider those people peers. For example, the leader of our public relations firm is a female CEO and her company is about the same size as mine and serves the same customer base. She represents me, but she's also a close personal friend and business associate. We share a passion for the industry and advancing our clients' best interests, and therefore keep an open dialogue about non-confidential but mutually interesting industry developments we individually learn about.

When I first founded my company, I decided that female owners of similar businesses who call on the same customers should know and recommend each other as opportunities present. Women are great at spreading good news, and we all had achieved "trusted, valued partner status" amongst our own customer base. I decided to host a full day meeting at the local and beautiful Rancho Valencia Spa, and invited these female CEOs and business owners to attend. They all called on the same biotech companies, even though their businesses sold totally different services like leadership development programs, relocation services, real estate, financial services, legal services, etc. They were all female business owners, and were invited for a relaxing day and an opportunity to meet new people and to hear one another's pitches.

Over the course of the day, we listened to everyone's elevator pitch and discussed how to identify opportunities for each other and therefore better support each other. We wanted to be able to recognize and pass on opportunities that another woman's business could realize. That was the secret of my success in San Diego: putting together referral relationships where nobody gets paid a finder's fee.

In the beginning, it was just executive women running their own companies who I believed needed to know each other. But it lasted because we knew everyone was the best at what they did and wanted to help one another. Instead of mentors and mentees, it became a network of advisors, and we even list them on our website to formalize it further. We provide our customers a full service and happily connect them with other service providers we recommend. The core premise is that we're peers who want to help each other, while also helping our customers.

Another way to find mentors and advisors is through participation on boards for various organizations, events, and causes. I'm on multiple nonprofit boards because of my belief in giving back and leaving the world a better place through my business. The people that serve with me on these boards are, again, cross-functional people who have been hugely instrumental in building local awareness around what we do. I consider them another group of advisors, as well as another referral network.

For instance, a close friend and colleague of mine is now the public relations leader at Scripps Hospital, and is a conduit to many other things I'm currently involved with in the community. She was the person who nominated me to the board of LEAD San Diego, a leadership organization for developing executives. Additionally, the Editor-in-Chief for the San Diego Business Journal is also on the board of LEAD San Diego with me. Recently, he was writing a list of the top 500 influencers in San Diego for an annual publication and asked me to help suggest some biotech leaders as part of his research. Surprisingly, he decided to include me in the Top 500 book, for which I'm very thankful. More importantly, he and I have a lot of common interests, and he wanted to learn all about the biotech crowd and how to develop relationships with them. I was happy to introduce him, and we're continuing to build our networks together. The Business Journal considers me a good source for their articles, and I'm happy to share all of the insights I have when they call. The best business relationships are "win/win" and mutually beneficial.

DON'T FORGET YOUR NON-BUSINESS FRIENDS

I have many friends that have nothing to do with my industry, and I think that's a really important circle to have. Different perspectives and viewpoints provide different insights and, therefore, different ways of attacking the same old problems. There's something to be said about a fresh pair of eyes.

We don't have all of the answers to advancing our careers or navigating tough business issues inside of ourselves. Yes, you can read books, but you're not bouncing ideas off of anyone else if that's all you do. Honestly, you need to get people to challenge your assumptions and challenge the things you think are good ideas. You're going to get a variety of viewpoints as you do that. And your point of view is not always the right one—I know we've all had that experience. Someone else may come up with a better idea than you had—even without intimate knowledge of your industry. And that's bound to happen to you every day. Being a growth-minded person will help you embrace this feedback, no matter the source.

I learned about the concept of being growth-minded from a research psychologist named Eve Grodnitsky, PhD, who has a terrific YouTube talk called *"How Mindset Can Transform Your Business and Life."* Eve is an impressive speaker, having studied both developing insight and the power of mindset, so I engaged her to talk to my team as a motivational speaker. It was very beneficial because everybody wants to think of themselves as growth-minded, but they may not actually be showing up that way in the workplace. It has nothing to do with what you think about yourself but how you act.

To illustrate this, we each took a blank piece of paper and drew a horizontal line through the center. On the right side we wrote "Growth Mindset," and on the left we wrote "Fixed Mindset." Each team member was instructed to write their name on top of the page and pass it around to their peers. Each peer was instructed to write their name along the horizontal axis on your page as to where they felt your mindset fell along the continuum—where you showed up for them.

When your paper was returned to you, you quickly learned which type of mindset you had been exhibiting in the workplace by the location of the marks. Fixed-minded people stood out in everyone's minds because they showed up every day acting like they knew everything already. Fixed minded people believe they are "born with all the cards" and their job is to look smart. Typically, they prefer not to seek any feedback from anyone, because feedback is painful to them. We see this a lot in certain professions, where people believe (or at least give the impression to others around them) that they know everything and don't welcome feedback. Unfortunately, if this is you, it may not be how you actually feel or think, but it's the aura you're giving off. If you're not open to hearing what others think, you will appear to be fixed-minded instead of having an open mind about receiving the feedback necessary for personal growth.

To growth-minded people, feedback is appreciated and considered valuable because it helps them grow—it is welcomed and doesn't feel like a knife in the back. If someone gives you feedback and it does feel very painful, then you are likely showing up as a fixed-minded person to those around you. Interestingly, according to the University of North Carolina's Kenan-Flagler Business School, 65 percent of the population exhibit fixed-mindset behaviors in their interactions.

It's important that you learn to escape that mindset and begin to really value all feedback. No matter how hard it is for you to receive it in the moment, it will serve you well to learn to say, "Thank you very much. I take feedback very seriously, and I appreciate your input." They felt it important to share it with you, which is worth respecting. At a minimum I'd encourage you to at least think about what they said and try to incorporate it going forward if it's warranted upon deeper reflection.

The most impressive executives outwardly exhibit a growth mindset and thank people for their input and feedback—no matter how hard it may be. That's the most professional, executive thing you can do: thank them and then go and think about it. Later, you can return for further non-confrontational conversation: "I was really trying to get to the bottom of why you felt this way about me and this is what I'm thinking, because I want to learn from this and improve." Being balanced and gracefully accepting feedback is stage one.

Yes, it's hard. But your friends, and especially your mentors, are going to give you the tough love you need. You pay your coaches to give you tough love, but they may not always give it to you for fear you might fire them for being harsh. You don't have all the answers and without talking to someone outside yourself, you'll never have those worthwhile conversations—you'll be too easy or too hard on yourself, neither of which is beneficial.

Be brave enough to ask for feedback.

ACTION ITEMS:

- **Take inventory:** List the key individuals in your life who are already your mentors.

- **Make a list of potential future mentors:** Leverage your network for ideas and possible inroads.

- **Create a specific action plan to meet future mentors:** Request necessary connections through your current network.

- **Explore hiring a career coach:** Clearly define what you're trying to accomplish.

- **Research:** Discover and interview at least three different career coaches.

- **Continually seek out different perspectives:** Don't forget your non-business friends.

- **Ask for feedback:** Request it whenever you can and practice receiving it gracefully.

CREATE YOUR CAREER MAP

Long before you land your first executive role, you need to be thinking about your career trajectory. Making smart choices along the way primes you for taking that first executive step. The two worst things you can do is choose bad companies along the way and make too many detours on your career path by "accident."

Poor company choices and too many career detours can happen for any number of reasons, but they almost all stem from an improper evaluation of opportunities and companies at the onset. Assess each business opportunity before you make the leap into employment. I see this often with women in board situations—many women just want to be on boards. They raise their hand for everything and say, "Just call me for any board opportunity." Remember, you will be representing the company and will be responsible for its performance, so as with all jobs, you should be highly selective and critical. Your time is your main asset, so spend it wisely and with intention as you progress your career.

The *company* you choose to work for is important and not just the position. Vigorously research your local landscape and find the five to ten companies where you would add extreme value. Find out everything you can about their business practices, including speaking to current and past employees, to discern if you'd like to be involved in their company's vision and mission. Narrow it down to just the ones that sit best with you. Then, make a move. Don't just wait for your phone to ring. Any companies who are reaching out to you are thinking about their best interest, not yours. Reach out to those companies that are the best fit for your career aspirations and tell them how you can add value to their business. Call the CEO and offer to buy him or her coffee. Show how you are aligned with their culture and mission with a focus on sharing specific ideas you have to enhance their success.

START WITH A PLAN

Along your career path, about 75 percent of your energy should be directed to doing your day job exceptionally well, while at least 25 percent should be devoted to your own career development. Employers may offer some programs, however they won't actually do this part for you. Many people feel like their employer owes it to them, or they expect that they will provide a career path document. But that's simply not true. You have to overdeliver, create your own value, and take charge of your own career development.

Spend one afternoon every week specifically planning your career advancement strategy. Warren Buffett and Bill Gates both make time to plan and give themselves time to think—it's critical to their success. Follow their lead and consistently schedule time to plan the next step in your career—not just when you feel a transition is imminent or long overdue.

Let's dive deeper into the planning time every woman needs to have on her calendar.

One afternoon per week should be devoted to career planning, but two hours each day should go to general self-development.

How can you use that time productively?

Typically, I schedule my self-development time in the afternoons; my mornings are extremely busy with customer appointments across different time zones. Use your peak time—when you have the highest energy—to meet all the demands of your employer, speak with customers or hold meetings. It's my experience these activities tend to slow down a little bit in the late afternoon, around 3pm to 5pm. Try to block that window as "thinking and planning time" in your calendar.

If it sounds extreme to do it every day, start with at least three days per week. As I said before, I believe women should spend 25 percent of their time planning and 75 percent of their time doing their current job. You're going to get conflicts every now and then; sometimes you're going to accept a meeting that runs into your private time. But don't take it off of your calendar—it's a commitment to yourself to keep doing it, and you need the constant reminder until it becomes a habit.

When I catch a glimpse of someone's calendar and they have scheduled thinking time, I can't help but respect them immensely for it. It's remarkable and amazing when a person can keep this commitment to themselves and their development. It isn't just time to kick back and take a nap under your desk—it's serious thought about strategy and the trajectory of your professional career.

Split your thinking time into a 50/50 mix of short and long-term goals. Ask yourself: "What do I think is really possible within a one-year time frame, and what is really possible within a five-year time frame?" The short-term planning encompasses the critically important things you're going to get done between now and the end of the year. It expands to looking ahead to the upcoming year on the horizon and also involves reassessing the present. Develop a personal plan of achievement for what you want to get done for yourself this year. Set it up at the beginning of the year, check on it periodically, and then reframe as necessary.

Throughout the planning process, you should always be asking yourself: "Am I doing all of the things I can think of to move me personally forward while still helping to move my employer's goals forward?" If you fail to appreciate what is going to move the needle for your employer, you're never going to go anywhere at that company. Part of your annual planning process should involve making advances at your current job. Most importantly, how can you add value to *your employer this year*? What can you do that really demonstrates *your value to this company?* As you create value, you have to leverage that value to create upward mobility for yourself.

An integral part of long-term planning is deciding on a succession process. How do you develop the people that are coming up behind you? Who do you have? How can you begin to build a bridge for yourself? If your aspiration is to go into next level leadership, what kind of leadership training and mentors do you need? What kind of mentor do you need to be for your replacement? You want to propose the answers to those questions to your manager and clearly ask for what you want: "I really want to learn to lead a team—how I can help you do that, while learning in the process?"

If they don't want to invest in you, go out and buy that leadership program for yourself. Just tell them you're taking paid time off and go for it. You wouldn't believe the difference putting out effort to gain leadership skills makes in an employer's opinion of you. First of all, you're investing in yourself, taking your own personal time, and you'll start to show up like a different person as your program inspires you. Whether it's an academic program like an MBA or some community college courses, you can always try asking your employer if they're able to support you. A lot of employers can't and won't, but it's important to at the very least ask. But if you take it upon yourself to do this and your behavior begins to change the workplace, you've really set yourself up for success.

A woman who was working for me as an administrative assistant took a leadership program and it changed her world—it was like she became a different version of herself altogether. Because I saw this change, I joined the leadership organization's board and I stand fully behind their work. I have been a speaker in their courses, and our company sponsors their Innovation Awards annually. I still thank that employee for getting me involved with LEAD San Diego. You have to take initiative because it demonstrates to your employer that you believe in yourself and your own personal and professional development. If they see you investing in yourself on a regular basis, they'll know you truly care about leadership and that you take your personal career advancement seriously.

LEAD San Diego has since been acquired by San Diego's Chamber of Commerce and is a brilliant group with a number of different programs for executive development. The entry level program my administrative assistant completed is called "Impact," which introduces you to influential people and teaches you from the lessons the leaders around you learned. When my employee first brought it up to me, I was a bit biased against it, thinking, *We work with leaders all day every day. There are already plenty of leaders here for you to learn from.* But then I realized I was the one working directly with leaders, not my team. And it turned out to be very valuable to her. In the process, I learned an important lesson: when someone asks for this type of investment from their employer, they'll learn something meaningful from it and it will have great long-term effects. She was proud that I took the time to get involved at the top of the organization, and I really began making a difference for other aspiring executives in need of these trainings and opportunities. As I briefly mentioned earlier, I've served alongside some incredible people on the board, and I am grateful for each and every opportunity the organization has brought forth in my life.

If you're reading this book, you are already a high-potential individual and your company should be investing in you. It may not always be possible, and you shouldn't get disappointed, but do be willing to invest in yourself and they'll learn from watching you take the lead.

MAP YOUR PROGRESSION

Have a one-year and a five-year plan for yourself that you refresh every year as you would a business plan. You are developing a business: the business of your career. It's really hard to see ten, twenty, thirty years in the future, but you can definitely think about five. And if you're having a hard time with five, start with three. The point is to start mapping out your future toward accomplishing your big stretch goal.

Once a year, sit down and re-map your course. Talk about strategies and tactics with your mentor or whomever you're working on your career plan with. Ask yourself what you need to learn this year to fast forward your career. What big goal is on your distant horizon? That goal becomes the North Star guiding your way. What will you need to do to get there from where you are today?

Also use this once-a-year re-map as a time of reflection. What did you accomplish this past year? List those accomplishments and think of them as tools you're putting in your tool belt to move you towards your big North Star goal. If you manage your career in this way, if you annually write smart goals for yourself and create accountability around what you're going to learn, the strategies and goals you set out for yourself will be in manageable bite-sized pieces. Once you accomplish those, at the end of the year as you reflect on the previous period, think about the next year, re-calibrate, and adjust your five-year plan accordingly.

As you go through each year, and throughout your career, that horizon will likely change—and that's okay. It's hard to predict with 100 percent accuracy what you'll need when you set out, and that's why you re-calibrate. When they graduate, very few people know what they're going to be when they grow up. But you can plan a five-year career path of what you think you'd like to be in that instant. And as I said before, if you're more comfortable with three years, start there.

Career planning and mapping, as we've discussed, is critically important when you're interviewing for a position. You want to be perceived as someone who has a plan, and having a plan makes each choice you make intentional. Don't navigate your career randomly. Each step you take should have a reason behind it. You will be forever employable because you are a planned and thoughtful person collecting experiences for your tool belt—no matter how far you aspire to go in your career. My guess, since you're reading this, is that you want to be a wildly successful executive. We've talked about the definitions of success, and it varies for everyone, but there is some sort of career goal that you specifically aspire to reach. And you can. And even if and when you find yourself in a position that's not for you, don't despair. I've been there, too.

In my case, I was fortunate that my degree allowed me to land a job immediately upon graduation. But soon after donning the white coat, I knew that being a medical technologist in a laboratory wasn't the right fit for me. From a career planning standpoint, I realized that my strengths would make me suitable for sales. And I wanted to learn sales. My objective became to do as much toward learning sales as I could while I was in this laboratory role.

In the beginning, I earned the opportunity to manage people at multiple sites and to spend time with my head of sales mentor. There was a salesperson assigned to my region, and I wanted to learn as much as I could from him. Part of that was learning customer service—a big aspect of being successful at sales. And between this self-imposed internship and reading a lot of books about how to sell, I felt prepared. I didn't have any practical experience per se, but when the same employer moved me to a different state, I told them I wanted to switch to sales.

"Laboratory employees don't make good sales people," I was told.

"I plan to try," I replied. "I really need to do this—it's a growth opportunity for me."

My current employer didn't understand, so I thought long and hard about it, then gathered the courage to "cold call" the VP of Sales in person at a competitor laboratory.

And the next company listened. They acknowledged my passion and drive by choosing to support me and give me the chance to try my hand at sales. Making that decision ended up benefiting them because I was able to bring value to the company by doing something I wanted to do, and doing it well. I am forever grateful to my first sales leader and the company for taking a chance on me.

PURSUING YOUR PASSION PLACE

If you're someone who's trying to progress your career, you'll need to make a plan, stick to it, and find a company willing to help you realize your goals.

I had to learn the sales process to achieve it—that's where a mentor, reading books, and taking classes came in handy. And when I sat down with myself at the end of that first year to reflect, I thought, *What do I need to learn now to be a Sales Manager?*

That was my annual self-audit in practice. I re-calibrated my goal from Salesperson to Sales Manager; it was the next natural step in the progression of my career path. It took me a few years to get there, but I eventually earned a sales leadership role with five people reporting to me. And each year when I sat down to reflect, I kept looking for activities and things I could do to bring that goal closer. I became a student of leadership, and read self-improvement books constantly. I learned how to lead people from my mentor, and continued reading, learning, growing and preparing. It paid off: once I landed the role, we were recognized by our company as the best region for sales in the country within a very short period of time.

When there was a merger of that company with another company, I quickly realized the newly merged employees were not great salespeople. And, during the first merger meeting, I decided not to just teach them how to sell but to restructure the company's entire U.S. sales organization. Because I had already created value, when I proposed this idea, they trusted me to carry it out. I earned a promotion and relocated to the new site in North Carolina where I built a specialty sales force. As you move through your career, you need to take chances to make career strides. I took a chance suggesting this idea, it panned out, and I learned how to build a team from the ground up—adding another tool to my tool belt.

After building this specialized sales organization, we started being approached by all kinds of companies wanting to partner with us to promote and sell their products—from large, multinational companies to small startups. Because I had already made my one-year plan, I knew my five-year goal involved working in a small entrepreneurial company. And I put myself in a position to receive that by proposing a new alliance management position to my boss. Using all of my sales strengths, I could work with all of these small biotech companies that came in to pitch us. My boss agreed, and I gained access to a broad field of interesting startups.

At that time, my aspiration was to see and begin to understand the inner-workings of a startup. I didn't know anything about startups or the business side of biotech companies, but I knew I wanted to find out. And getting to know both showed me I wanted to end up in a biotech startup company or a small entrepreneurial organization. When one of them recruited me, I evaluated the entire horizon and went for it—I made another move across the country to take a startup role. I wanted to be an executive at the table. I hadn't done that yet, and here was my chance to learn about startups from a leadership position.

Whenever you're in a larger organization, it's hard to claim the growth trajectory because the size of the company makes it difficult to pinpoint what truly made the difference. Starting at zero revenue in a startup, however, allowed me to generate sales growth data that I could claim: I was there on the roadshow, helped raise the money alongside the CEO, was an officer around the table, and I built a commercial organization from the ground up. I built it all, from sales to marketing, customer service, and reimbursement. But in the beginning, I had no idea how to do any of this.

I remember on the first day of that job, I had to write a marketing business plan. I had never written a business plan before, having been in sales most of my career. Instead of being overwhelmed, I just got some books to show me how to do it. Then, I wrote a business plan.

In order to grow, you have to step out of your comfort zone. Pursuit of growth is a quality that all female CEOs seem to exhibit. To me, everything I did was a constant quest for growth. I hadn't figured out I wanted to be a CEO quite yet, but I did figure out that I wanted to own the sales organization. And over three years and several novel products later, we built the company from zero to $30 million.

Once I achieved that, I felt I needed a new challenge.

There's a moment where you feel like you've done everything you can for a company and you still need to keep growing and learning even though you're stuck in the same role. There was no advancement short of being the CEO when I was the commercial leader. So, I made the decision to resign.

Next, I created a photography tour company as a startup CEO. At the time I was married to a wildlife photographer, and thought it would be really fun to build a company in that space. It was my first company build and after about a year, I thought to myself, *This is fun—but I can do this and another job at the same time.*

From my time at the first startup to the period after my resignation, I learned how to start a company from scratch, moved to setting up a photo tour business and art gallery from zero, and expanded into retail. All of these were things I had always aspired to try. After my great year of experimenting, I thought to myself, *What am I really, really good at? What do I really love to do?*

I had always loved helping people advance their careers. It was always my favorite part of sales leadership. I also loved applying my negotiation skills and using my industry knowledge, plus earning the good money I had become accustomed to. I realized there was only one career that combined all four things—executive search!

At that moment, away from my core industry of sales, I committed to myself that I really wanted to be in executive search. After cold calling, applying to and interviewing with multiple search firms, I had an offer from one search firm; in parallel, I was also being recruited by a big, multinational organization for a GM-level role. I ultimately chose the global GM opportunity because I felt I would be more valuable as a multinational operating executive, but the desire to join a search firm stayed firmly planted in the back of my mind.

For three years, I worked in the global GM role, and I'm glad I did. But after postponing my happiness to gain that level of experience, I then knew it was time to finally go into search. As it turned out, the network I had just built was the exact network I needed for my next move.

One of my greatest professional accomplishments is building a very loyal and strong global network. As a result, I was able to quickly build more customer relationships while learning the ropes of executive search. I started out working for someone else to learn the field, similar to how I handled learning sales by jumping in with the help of someone more experienced than I was in that area. The executive search role immediately possessed me—I was able to manage a team while working with customers and selling all day. I instantly knew that I was in the right spot.

In two short years, we doubled the San Francisco-based business' revenue with the same number of people. As I learned this new industry, I fell more and more in love with it. But to build it the way I wanted to build it, I realized I would need to start my own company. It needed to be a very significant and substantial company to be successful in the executive search sphere, and because I had formed a company before I wasn't afraid of doing exactly that. In fact, I was excited. So I stepped away from my first search mentor and founded my own search firm, headquartered in San Diego. And it has been the best decision I've ever made. Later, I acquired the practice I originally managed in San Francisco and reunited with my original team.

Now I'm eight years into that journey, and I've learned that eight years is a good amount of time to build a company, optimize performance, and create multiple success stories. I was able to get the right amazing people around the table which made it all possible. Today, I have 20+ employees, four of whom I worked with 15-20 years prior, who followed me here from biotech—and most of my employees have stayed with me since I first started in search. So what am I most proud of? Building the company, engaging the hearts and minds of the team, driving revenue from zero to multi-millions, and most importantly working with really incredible people as candidates, customers, and trusted employees.

After you've established your career, it's important to continue setting goals. Nowadays, I really want to serve on more boards and use everything I've created for good. I currently serve on three non-profit boards, and aspire to join public company boards. I'll continue to be an owner in my business, but as it matures I will have more time for other projects. I still have a frustrated artist and musician within: you're never done learning, growing, and determining.

Always be filling your plan with things you're trying to learn along the way. Then, make time to learn those things, and—of course—make plans to give back.

ORGANIZING YOUR ACCOMPLISHMENTS

Companies don't just need CEOs—they need every level of team member within the organization. They need operations, research, product development, sales, marketing, services—they need everything. And global companies need all of these positions, too. Putting the pieces of those different jobs together is a journey. As you learn the intricacies of all of those different pieces, you learn how to fit them together. This is the preparation you need to become a CEO.

When you interview for a CEO position, the most important thing is to be able to recount your career map and to include a summary of what you actually learned at each position. You will want to add in how you can bring those skills to your next role. People want accomplishments that are measurable and can be spelled out. The number one place people go wrong is not characterizing their accomplishments as goals they achieved through quantifiable means. Spend time figuring out what exactly you did to reach that accomplishment and capture it on your resume. This way, it's easier for you to explain all of it in a concise, organized fashion.

To begin creating your resume, start wherever you are along your journey and work backwards. Just as you think forward five years, you have to be aware of your retrospective map of the past five years, too. List every job, the reason you took it (even if it was just to feed yourself when you were younger), and what you learned from it. When you first start interviewing for big jobs, you have to claim the skills you learned and be able to verbalize them.

In high school, I was a dental assistant in the afternoon after finishing my classes. How would I illustrate that on a resume? Dental assistant would be the title, but what I actually learned was that the Dentist I worked for was a really weak leader. Sometimes you can learn negative lessons but you need to learn to spin them in a positive way. It was probably the worst working environment I have ever seen and I told him as much. But he appreciated the feedback. And he ended up hiring me again when I was in college because as a result of my feedback, he changed his leadership style. On my resume, I would put that I learned the value of feedback in conflict resolution and creating a more hospitable work environment for myself and the team around me.

Every summer, I was a server in a restaurant, which gave me customer service experience. I took those jobs to pay for college, but I quickly learned how to upsell my customers. Everything I've done since has been selling in some form or another. Everyone should wait tables for a crash course in people skills, multi-tasking, memory, and discipline. It's one of the hardest jobs there is, but it's foundational for the development of many important, key skills.

Serving, like sales, is one of those careers where the better you are at it and the harder you work, the more money you can make. I treated it as my career rather than just doing something to make ends meet, and this mindset shift set me up to work hard and be successful. That earning structure also predisposed me to seek opportunities in sales. When I ended up as a medical technologist in a lab, I was disappointed it didn't have the same paradigm; I had already learned that I like to be paid proportionally to my effort. Instead, at the lab I was trading time for money. Early on, I recognized the distinction between my different jobs and which ones I preferred: those where I was rewarded for amazing effort. Knowing this about myself added exponential possibility. Today, even executive search is commission driven, and I love the model and the talent it attracts.

The ideal amount of time to spend in a company is three years and the longest is probably eight years. Three to eight years is the range of reasonably long tenures during which you can accrue and own your accomplishments. If you come and go too quickly, within one or two years, it becomes difficult to demonstrate what you've done. Again, sometimes moves happen accidentally: you get recruited or promoted externally. But you have to be careful about making too many moves or you can't claim anything. Employers will say, "Yes, you held the title, but what did you actually do? You weren't even there when the product launched or when the sales happened." Stay long enough to achieve some accomplishments that you can actually be proud of before you go on to the next position. And don't leave too soon—leaving too soon precludes you from learning everything you could learn. Everyone has a different cycle for when they need a new challenge. But make sure you have some accomplishments first—don't leave too soon.

Following your path may require many moves, and your resume will reflect this. You'll want to draw your career on paper before you write your resume and organize your thoughts. Figure 2.0 shows a sample Career Map where you'll note all of the moves you've made and distinguish whether each one was a physical move or a move from one company to the next.

These moves indicate someone who has managed their career thoughtfully. Moves show you are hungry to keep learning, growing, and adding to your tool belt. And you need to keep doing these things to increase your value. There's nothing wrong with staying on a flat career path your entire life, but if you're really trying to advance your career, you have to collect many accomplishments. The accomplishments and value you added to your employer are what will get you

FIGURE 2.0

MOVE - CO., PROMOTION, PHYSICAL?	WHERE?	NEW POSITION COMPANY BOARD	WHY?	ACCOMPLISHMENT(S)

*VISIT WWW.ROBINTOFT.COM/TOOLS TO DOWNLOAD A COPY OF THIS TEMPLATE

the raise—not your tenure or demands.

Column one in the Career Map will show your moves as discussed above. The next column will be your timeline by year. For me, my moves ended up being about three years apart once I gathered enough data and history to see the pattern. I've discovered that is my window to learn what I need to learn before thinking that I need a new challenge.

The next column over is the position you held followed by the reason you accepted it and what you hoped to learn from it. When you're filling this out, you'll want to think back just prior to getting hired for each job. Really look at the aspiration or motivation that was inherent in that decision. The next column of your sheet lists your accomplishments and your final column should list what you actually learned from each position. That way, you have your expectations and reality accounted for. This is the framework for your perfect resume right here.

Typically a resume is a date, company, job title, and list of duties. But what you did needs to be *quantifiable* and must be *significant*. Frame it in such a way that highlights skills applicable to the job you're applying for. When you begin to do that, you are ready for hire. Anybody who plans this way is a really attractive candidate because it demonstrates strategy, a strategic plan and accounting of yourself.

INHERENT SKILLS & YOUR RESUME

When it comes to listing specific things you learned from a position, don't neglect the "inherent skills." These are the skills that come naturally from performing a specific function. For example, a sales rep inherently learns the sales process. They're obvious lines on your resume, but they're important to include.

Let's use my own Career Map as a case study (see Figure 3.0).

From this, let's examine my position as Managing Director of Executive Search. If we look at the skills that are inherent in that position, we come up with "building a customer base." In order to be successful in this role, I had to identify prospective clients, develop them into viable leads, present our company to them, and convince them to work with us. Essentially, you're getting someone to sign on for a service and you're building a map of clients.

Now you can see how this actually translates into the development of your resume. This map can be transformed into your resume—it is in essence your resume creator.

Most people don't create a resume properly because they're just

FIGURE 3.0

MOVE - CO., PROMOTION, PHYSICAL?	WHERE?	NEW POSITION COMPANY BOARD	WHY?	ACCOMPLISHMENT(S)
2018 - Physical Move	San Francisco	CEO, Toft Group WE CAN	Building new co./ brand to develop diversity talent pool	Established WE CAN network in San Fran and San Diego, published book for executive women, established strong PR & speaking engagements
2017 - New Co.	San Diego	CEO, Real Estate Investment Company	Learn about real estate & build co. as investment	Acquired 4 properties and established strong rental income
2010 - New Co.	San Diego	CEO, Toft Group Executive Search	Build a recruiting company from the ground up	Scaled revenue from $0-9M over 8 years, built team of 20 in 3 cities, Won Woman of the Year in San Diego and Athena Top Company, Increased brand awareness & reputation
2006 - Physical Move/ New Co.	San Diego	Managing Director, Executive Search	Learn New Industry (Executive Search)	Earned top performing office nationally out of 50 offices in first year
2005 - Promo-tion	San Francisco	SVP Commercial. Ops	Learn Global Executive Team leadership	Built Global Network for commercialization of novel products, attended HI Potential Leadership Program in Switzerland
2003 - Moved Companies	San Francisco	VP Commercial Operations	Regional Executive Team	Built and led local marketing team, earned SVP & Officer
2001 - Moved Companies/ New Co.	San Francisco	CEO, Photography Tour & Gallery Company	Learn New Industry (Photography); Build first co.	Established & built profitable photo tour company; Opened Photographic Gallery
1998 - Moved Companies/ New Co./ Physical Move	San Francisco	VP Sales & Marketing, Start-up	Learn about Start-up and leading Marketing (broader scope)	Drafted start-up business plan, served on executive team, scaled revenue from $0-30M. Established infrastructure for 4 functions (hired, trained, and lead areas)

MOVE - CO., PROMOTION, PHYSICAL?	WHERE?	NEW POSITION COMPANY BOARD	WHY?	ACCOMPLISHMENT(S)
1997 - Promotion	North Carolina	Associate VP Alliances	Learn negotiation and business development	Negotiated multiple BD deals with partners, bringing high value to company
1995 - Physical Move & Promotion	North Carolina	Associate VP Specialty Sales	Build specialty sales organization & learn oncology	Built new team - delivered 10-15% growth annually
1993 - Promotion	San Diego	Sales Manager	Leadership - Manage a Sales Team	Recruited & developed a strong team; For all 3 years, won top region in country
1990 - Moved Companies/ Physical Move	San Diego	Sales Reresentative	Learn Sales Process	Top Performer within 400+ person sales organization, $1M sales in first year, won many awards
1987 - Physical Move & Promotion	Hawaii	Laboratory Manager & University Instructor	Leadership/ Management of Teams & Teaching	Managed labs & multiple sites while teaching classes
1983 - First Career	Michigan	Medical Technologist - Individual Contributor	Broad learning opportunities - First Career	Mastered individual contributor role, ultimately managed small team

listing jobs instead of what they actually learned and accomplished. If a person can create her timeline and map her progress, a resume can easily be fashioned from it. Put your five-year horizon at the top, and then you have your North Star directing everything.

You have to be prepared for the very standard question, "What's your five-year plan?" when you're interviewing. If you don't have a five-year plan, your interview will not go well. But given that you will have a five-year plan after having read this book, the next question becomes "How much or how little of the plan do you divulge to the potential employer?" Having a career goal is expected—you should say something that's authentic, but, if for whatever reason, it doesn't synchronize with the job you're trying to get, be careful. Be as direct as possible and tell them your aspiration. For instance, if I were striving for CEO in the next five years, I would tell them I really want to learn to be a CEO in the next five years and that's the path I'm on. There's nothing wrong with saying that. They expect you to have something compelling to say when asked about your five-year plan.

If you say, "I hope to be a CEO one day," they'll probably reply, "Well, do you think this is on the path?" A great way to preemptively answer that question is by leading with how this position fits into your plan and goals. "I'm striving to be a CEO one day, and I'm interested in this job as a way to learn business development and to transition to the commercial area. I've been operating in a manufacturing function up until this point, and I know I'm going to be good in a commercial role for these reasons: [insert reference to your accomplishments and inherent skills to prove you deliver]." Some aggressive moves are necessary while you are pursuing your North Star goal—you can see I did those types of tactics a lot. But you know when you need to do them and you shouldn't be afraid. You've been successful to date. You can do anything.

If we're revisiting your Career Map every year and re-calibrating it to your North Star, you'll want to update it and keep it current. One year into the process means you still have a ways to go towards your North Star goal. There's still a lot of that mountain to climb, but what do you need to do to reach the next peak? If your pursuit is generally the same, the second year on your path should include a revenue objective and a "size of the company" objective. The intent is to form a game plan for the next year right now by setting up these annual goals for yourself.

By setting these goals, you can achieve real accomplishments to add to your resume and Career Map. For example, you may say, "I want to generate $2 million in revenue and I want to lead a team of five people." All of the things that you've done in your business plan or in your personal goal plan build your credibility and your value. And your value is absolutely conditional upon accomplishments— anyone who thinks otherwise is not playing the same game that everyone else is playing. To get paid, you have to have accomplishments or they're not going to give you escalation of your salary. Take these accomplishments to the next employer to demonstrate your worth and value to come in at the right level. Value has nothing to do with how long you've been in a job or which jobs you've had—it's about what you achieved and what skills you learned.

If you're on an annual planning calendar wherever you're working, I would say the end of the year is the best time for this type of assessment of yourself and your career plan. I love the week between Christmas and the New Year because nearly everybody is winding down and forming resolutions for the upcoming year ahead. You can also clearly see how the company you work for performed. If revenue is one of your drivers, you may be able to gauge what your actual revenue contribution for the year was. And it's the perfect time to be thinking about the year to come. Just take time for yourself and reflect. And if you're consistently following your path, it's going to be easy to refresh it and move the bar a little bit forward every year. It's not Herculean at all, because you're simply doing small revisions every year during your annual re-assessment.

Your annual re-assess covers your business objectives, goals, strategies, and tactics. Write down your tactics and commit to them—and to yourself. I would physically go outside to do this exercise. It might seem silly, but it's freeing and gives you a fresh, energized perspective. Spend an entire day out in nature, planning for yourself. Bring your plan and write everything down: your goals, strategies, and tactics. When you have a goal, you can break it into strategy and tactics to accomplish it—that's a business plan. These tactics are things you can physically do and deliver for yourself by the end of the year. Review it quarterly, just as you do at the end of the quarter with your company, to make sure you're on track. This way, you won't be surprised at the big end-of-year re-assess.

Ask yourself, "How am I doing against my plan?" If you're falling short of your plan, I would suggest not adjusting it, but simply doubling down on doing whatever it takes to make it happen. Make yourself the priority and make this learning happen. It's very impressive if you're a mid-career, aspiring executive and you take this to your boss and review your plan with them. I would personally be wildly impressed if my people shared their career aspirations and plans with me. We, as employers, tend to do that for people at work by saying, "These are going to be your goals for next year," rather than allowing them to originate and present their own goals. Someone who does it on their own, however—that's a very impressive way to demonstrate you are seeking continued career growth and shows tremendous initiative.

When you take it upon yourself to set your own goals it demonstrates to your leader that you have a plan, you're aspirational, you need continued growth, and you deserve professional development. It shows you have the discipline to plan annually and you're communicating what you'd like to do next. Now, they have that seed planted in their mind. If you have a good relationship, which I hope you do with your boss, then they know you need a growth opportunity. Once they understand this, most great bosses will try to find it for you. You've created value and they don't want to lose you. That's a powerful, impactful way to guide your career after you've written your plan. Just have an annual sit-down with your boss before the year kicks off. Create a document with clear goals and tactics, personally review it, commit to it, put a signature line at the bottom and sign off on it, and then take it to your boss and review and have her or him do the same.

If all of my people did that with me, I would be thrilled because it makes my job so much easier. It can be hard because you're still aspiring, but it also effectively assures them you're not dissatisfied—you just need consistent growth and learning opportunities.

If you and your boss both mutually agree that your plan is not achievable within the organization, then you will need to address that. Should you adjust your plan to align with what you could accomplish within that particular company? I would advocate against that and perhaps look at going elsewhere to meet your goals. If you can't get the growth or learning you aspire to in the next five years, or even the next year, I think you should resign your position and go somewhere that will offer those opportunities. In my experience leading an executive search firm, the number one reason we see people change jobs is lack of career progression or growth.

If your company has performance reviews already built into its cycle, align your mapping cycle with the performance review cycle. Use your time to review what you think you need to learn and be ready to discuss it with your superiors. By doing this, you're able to leverage help in the achievement of your goals by having the company commit to your progress.

ACTION ITEMS:

- **Fully assess each business opportunity:** Examine each one carefully before you make the leap into employment, including Board of Director roles.

- **Research your local landscape:** List companies where you would add extreme value.

- **Reach out:** Make contact with the shortlist of companies that are the best fit for your career aspirations; tell the CEO how you can add value.

- **Schedule 4-6 hours of career planning time per week:** Make sure it's on your calendar and treat it just as you would any other business appointment.

- **Commit to an annual career development goal:** Review your progress against it quarterly and course correct when necessary.

- **Create your succession plan:** Identify the people you will develop to succeed you.

- **Identify a career development course or seminar:** Invest in yourself and attend, even if your employer will not sponsor you.

- **Create your Career Map:** Go to www.robintoft.com/tools and download the Career Map template. Include clear accomplishments in each role as a foundation for your resume.

- **Review your Career Map and annual goals:** Schedule time with your manager and jointly agree upon your annual career development plan.

THE SIX PHASES OF CAREER DEVELOPMENT

In my experience, having interviewed thousands of executives, it is clear that finding your perfect career is rarely a straight path—you go up one ladder and then you may need to climb down and go up another.

Your Career Map can be broken down into the six phases of career development: Pre-Career, Early Career, Emerging, Established, Mature, and Encore.

1. THE PRE-CAREER PHASE

Foundational careers establish you as an employed person in the world while you build skills and cultivate knowledge. These are typically miscellaneous jobs like waiting tables and general customer service roles. Pre-Career work experience builds the foundation for how you'll operate along your entire career path and helps you develop aspirations.

Once you realize you can actually get paid for tasks and start earning money, you'll establish an initial—typically minimal—amount of value for the first time. You'll begin to build some self-awareness around your own career likes, dislikes, and abilities, and learn that hard work is rewarded. These years are about trading time for money. The Pre-Career phase is often when academic training and internships come into play.

View this period of time as getting your "sea legs" and acclimating to the working world.

Many times the experience you gain during this phase is from a job, and not necessarily a career. This can be anything from odd jobs you were paid for as a kid all the way through the more formal jobs you worked at while going through post-secondary education.

2. THE EARLY CAREER PHASE

You move into Early Career when you enter the workforce in your first meaningful role or occupation. This is your foundational career that sets your trajectory. You may be doing what you studied in college or what's associated with your academic situation. You usually start doing what you thought you were going to do when you're fresh out of college, or give what you studied a test-run. Is this what you really are intended to be and/or do? It's either validating or will inspire you to change career focus. But you will only know when you show up and experience the workplace and expectations for the role firsthand. It may not be what you expected or even something you enjoy. You're trying out the career you thought you were going to have, and it's okay that most people don't choose correctly initially—really, they don't. As tedious as it may seem, trial and error is a hallmark of the Early Career stage. These years are about trading time for experiences.

Once you're in your foundational career you may decide that it's not your dream career. This happens often and you shouldn't worry—you now have a landscape view of other careers that are possible, even within the same company. There are often a wide variety of roles available, and most companies will allow you to try wearing a lot of hats, particularly if you join a startup. If you're in a large company, you can see an outside view of other positions within the organization. It is, however, important to shadow and interview people to figure it out and try to make a better decision as you progress. But if you haven't even done that, don't sweat it.

I'll confess that I didn't—I just took the classes I was interested in and studied hard to excel at them. And because of that, I didn't know what the job would be like. Sure enough, the job was not my ideal job whatsoever. From the moment I walked in and put on the white coat and looked into a microscope, I knew that was not what I should be doing. Had I done more upfront research and really tried to scout it out before I ended up there, I would have had an idea before I was already committed. For me, my first year in the laboratory was quite a challenge and I tried to make it work (probably for too long). It took me a number of years to transition out of it. I made the determination for myself that I was going to learn skills in that environment and then move on. I tried other career options, such as teaching laboratory medicine in a university setting rather than working in a lab, in an effort to move toward my passion for working with people. I ultimately saw sales from my laboratory job and thought, *I think I would enjoy promoting the company's services rather than actually being part of the execution and delivery model.*

As I referenced earlier, I've seen it often with attorneys. Law students are very uninformed of the realities of working within a legal practice. Often, they come out of law school and realize they don't actually like practicing law. That is why being an intern or job shadowing is paramount when you're in school—to ensure that when you get into a position, you've chosen the right career in the first place. But if you haven't had the opportunity to do internships during your Pre-Career education, the Early Career stage is the time.

I also interview many people like this in medicine. Maybe they had doctors in the family and went to medical school to carry on the tradition. When they got out, they realized they hated the redundancy of seeing patients for the same ailments. Some of those doctors evolved and later joined an industry setting where they could do medical affairs away from the actual practice of medicine. They don't have to see patients, but they have and can leverage their clinical knowledge.

In this phase, always ask yourself if you really love what you're doing. Or are you only doing it because you're good at it? If it's the latter, that doesn't mean you need to leave that company—you may love working there because of its culture or management team. But if you seek to be involved in entrepreneurial projects or a different aspect of that same company, then definitely plan the conversation with your boss and attempt to move into an area you enjoy.

Half the battle is to not be afraid of change and to have the courage to make a career pivot or change to utilize the skills you already have in your arsenal. If you know that you're in the wrong place, don't delay in navigating toward the right place for yourself by taking the next step in your career. Some people go right back into college and get advanced degrees and some choose to stick with employment and the working world—either is absolutely fine, depending upon your career objectives. And remember, you don't necessarily need to get an advanced degree. For instance, an MBA might help you with confidence and/or to build your business acumen, but unless you're in a specialized field, it is typically not required.

Unless you've chosen your perfect career with your first position (a definite rarity), people most often start in a completely different place and then make a lateral move into a role better suited for them. Accept the power of possibility and emerge in a new field and potentially the career of your dreams. If you try it out and really like it, stick with it and gather more accomplishments. And if you don't, rethink what attributes you want in a career and/or a company and make another move.

Don't stay in an unhappy or uninformed choice—you owe it to yourself to love your job. Many people will stay in a job they don't like because of other's expectations. Life is way too short to leave your key to happiness in someone else's pocket. At the end of the day, your career is where you spend forty hours a week—don't be disappointed with the function that you chose.

3. THE EMERGING CAREER PHASE

If Pre- and Early Career are your foundational career phases, then Emerging is when you've found your groove. Early Career is about trial and error, making mistakes, and finding the right environment in a meaningful occupation. Once you've found the right environment, you've moved into Emerging—you've figured out what you like and you're honing your skills. You're trying to become better and better at it because you've found your passion place and are refining your process. This involves building more successes along with meaningful value creation.

The hallmark of this phase is accruing achievements and making impressive accomplishments.

Often by this time you've determined your desired executive path, so you're looking for mentors, learning new skills, and honing the skills you already have. This career stage involves high intensity learning about industries and competitors, finding ways to create value, and seeking ways to maximize benefit for your employer. During this phase, you should begin seeking and requesting career development opportunities.

4. THE ESTABLISHED CAREER PHASE

Next you move from Emerging to becoming an Established executive in your chosen field.

The Established executive has created value in their career and has achieved numerous successes. They have the confidence of their peers, colleagues, and managers. They seek and ask for new opportunities—and receive them because they have a proven track record.

You'll soon reach the top of your game in this role and you will become very accomplished at it. Hitting a peak in this particular stage is normal, and it is exactly when you need to identify a new challenge.

As you become established in a particular role, the real challenge begins. You're going to cycle back through the Emerging, Establishing, and Maturing phases each time you change positions and as you get closer to your passion place. If you choose to change professions entirely, then you will have to go back to the Emerging phase in that new field.

For instance, I switched fields when I went to run a photographic gallery and then again when I pursued executive search. Both required completely new starts to learn the mechanics of the job, the landscape of the industry, the competitors, and how to create value. You can certainly apply your skills, but until you understand the new industry, you're still Emerging in the new role.

Once you reach the executive level, your experience is transferable within an industry—you will be Established in a variety of different companies at this level of expertise. If an Established executive switches companies within the same industry, he or she can typically parachute into different functions but stay at the executive level since they already understand the industry in which they're working. If you do decide to switch *companies AND industries*, you will need to return to Emerging. You can't be successful in a new industry or career until you learn how that field works. Part of succeeding in a competitive landscape is understanding who the players are and how you are going to position yourself or your company on the playing field. You'll most often cycle through the Emerging phase quickly and find yourself back at Established again before you know it. Then you can tell all of the pieces of your story—why you wrote each chapter and what you learned along the way.

Most people also have an ideal company stage that they prefer to be in and they feel less fulfilled on a daily basis when they are out of their ideal situation. For example, some executives with sales experience thrive in a mature company with products on market. If instead they join a very early stage company that is years away from selling products to customers and the company is instead involved in research and development only, it can be very frustrating for them. Surprisingly, I see CEOs and commercial leaders make this mistake time and time again. They haven't even paused to consider the potential frustration that may accompany not being able to talk to customers. Additionally, if you're entrepreneurial and stuck in an established company without any new product development, you'll be miserable and vice versa—people who prefer established companies don't typically do well in entrepreneurial environments. Either you're wired a certain way or you're not. And whichever way you're wired is okay, you just need to be conscious of it.

If you're an entrepreneur, you're a driven and committed person. After a mere three years in a startup you may feel like it has been twenty-one—the early years are the "dog years" of business. Time may seem to move differently, but for some executives it seems more joyful. Learn which career stage leaves you feeling the most inspired, and make an effort to stay in that stage as long and as often as possible. If continual creation is what provides you the most fulfillment, then continue to create. Revisiting a stage or learning a new industry is not "starting over," but simply a choice to return yourself to your ideal career stage in a different company.

If you love mature companies, then stay in a mature company where you can realize internal promotions instead of founding your own company and going through the dog years of business. A large multinational company may also be right for you. Several times in my career I worked in large multinational companies leading teams that were organized around specific projects to create value and solutions. Developing your career experiences within larger companies offers a different option for those who function better in more established companies. You just need to know what your role will entail and avoid choosing companies at the wrong stage, since it will become frustrating over time.

5. THE MATURE CAREER PHASE

As a mature executive, everything should be a well-oiled machine. Despite your consistency, you still seek accomplishments that continue to demonstrate value to your employer. At this stage, your value becomes the wisdom of leadership, decision-making, and the ability to guide people to achieve similar levels of excellence as a competent, capable leader.

Some mature female executives I know can parachute into any department, fully powered. These are the women I admire most, since they embody leadership in its most true sense. For instance, a Vice President of Project Management becomes Vice President of Regulatory Affairs. A Vice President of Strategic Planning becomes Vice President of Partnering. Because of your mature status within your company, you can move between functions. You are known internally to be a great leader and extremely knowledgeable in your industry. Leadership is a transferable skill that allows you to make parallel moves in your career.

As you work as a mature executive, your level of competence leads you to complete tasks more efficiently—you find yourself with more time and income. This then naturally leads to thoughts of succession and exit planning. You can stay in the mature executive phase as long as you're happy and inspired, but there are those who decide they need some new challenges. These people either find themselves back in Emerging—shaking up the snow globe in a whole new industry—or they do a lateral move to a different company and stay at the established level until they mature there.

Currently, I'm in a mature company that I built. I can remain there and find a new challenge within or I can make a decision to pursue another opportunity.

All executives, and particularly CEOs, should definitely create a succession plan for themselves and their companies since the company is reliant upon them for its success. At the executive level, it is imperative that you have a strong team to hand your responsibilities over to before making the personal decision to exit a company. Once you have trained your replacement, it is much easier to make a smooth transition and to follow your passion to the next opportunity.

Joining a non-profit can provide new inspiration and enhance your ability to change the world. Philanthropy doesn't have to wait until you reach the mature stage of your career, however having studied executive behavior it is my experience that most people wait until they're very confident in their disposable income levels. Keep in mind that donating money isn't the only form of philanthropy. When you're starting a new job or creating a new company, it can be all consuming and doesn't leave much spare time. Later, when you're more established in your career, you can donate your available time to non-profit boards and other pursuits that are important to you—time becomes another very valuable gift you can give. Your time is your most valuable asset, however, so donate it wisely to organizations that can truly appreciate your contribution.

6. THE ENCORE CAREER PHASE

Is there such a thing as retirement for the executive professional woman?

Personally, I don't like the word—I believe at this stage you're not retired, per se—you're just doing different things. Think of it as an "encore," and your chance to focus on what inspires you. Just as you may have been CEO of your household in an earlier part of your life, now you've moved into doing different things in this phase, too. I don't call it retirement because I have never seen a successful executive that actually fully retires. They always pursue some passion projects that they have, which is the hallmark of the retirement phase. For some people, identifying a passion project could be realizing they want to work on their golf game. It could be studying architecture, volunteering, producing art, playing piano, perfecting yoga poses, nothing, or everything.

To remain challenged many executives I work with opt to stay in business in some role—even if it's minor. Many choose to position themselves as an advisor, consultant, or a board member because they have true passion for the industry they have served throughout their career. There are all sorts of ways to leverage the strength you've acquired and not be a full-time employee. Piecing together a career out of three or four public board opportunities is really good income. Or, if you want to embrace retirement, private board opportunities can be very rewarding even if you're paid in equity. If you're already established and mature, the money's in the bank, so for most people it's less about the economics of the deal than now choosing where to spend your time and pay forward your knowledge. Be highly selective. Spend your time carefully since it is your most valuable asset. Use it to create a legacy.

Action Items:

- **Stage your career:** Decide which career stage you are currently in, and whether it is ideal for you at this time.
  - Pre-Career
  - Early Career
  - Emerging
  - Established
  - Mature
  - Encore

- **Be Fearless:** Don't be afraid to re-enter a stage as you transition to a new industry or start a new career path.

- **Give Back:** Donate your available time and money to board work (for profit or non-profit) and other pursuits that are important to you.

- **Plan your Encore:** Identify passion projects outside of work and foster them throughout your career with more emphasis during the Encore career stage.

CHARACTERISTICS OF THE FEMALE EXECUTIVE WARRIOR

The best leadership qualities to me are a growth mindset, a collaborative nature, an untiring work ethic, and good interpersonal skills. I develop people for a living, and these are all parts of the ideal leader I want them to become. Executives should be working to develop their employees, too, and lead by example. Beyond those mentioned above, there are other qualities important to have as a successful female executive. Let's explore them one by one.

DEFY THE CULT OF INDECISIVENESS

Women are often faulted for indecisiveness, but I would just say we like to debate and weigh our options. To generalize what I've seen in business, women prefer to be very accurate with our answers and decisions, making sure we fully understand and when asked to make a proposal, we follow up with a lot of questions for clarification. Immediate, decisive decision-making is not necessarily a sign of executive competency, but it is more often attributed to male executives who often make bold, less informed statements with confidence.

As an example, a boss may ask a female executive how many people and how much budget she needs to do a project. The woman typically asks as many questions as possible, then bids accurately— for instance, the project will require $6M dollars and need 20 new employees. A man is typically less detail driven and makes bolder statements—it will take $3M and only takes 10 people. The boss likes the male employee's decisiveness, confidence, and lower estimate. Unfortunately, the company didn't realize the woman's estimate was way more accurate for the project, which actually did take $6M and 20 employees. The retrospective was never done.

So the female executive should secure enough accurate information quickly to respond with confidence, and worry less about the retrospective analysis. Answer decisively with confidence, and substantiate with as many details as possible, realizing there will be more time to conduct more due diligence if she is selected to lead the project.

Additionally, be concise when approaching a challenge. When you are faced with a significant challenge in the workplace or in life, I suggest you always consider three different possible solutions. Fully evaluate all three possibilities with pros and cons, identify the best one, then present the problem, the three possibilities, and your proposed solution to your manager. She or he will appreciate that you have thoroughly considered all angles and are presenting a concise potential solution. A solutions-focused approach versus simply presenting a problem will accelerate your career.

SELF-CARE

If you find it a constant struggle to relax and achieve balance in your life, welcome to the club! You may be an extremist or an adrenaline junkie—that's how you prefer to operate. But how can you avoid the cycle of burnout? Schedule time for yourself to refresh and detox. Then, actually commit to do it.

Every single day, I set aside hours to walk my dogs in nature and plan additional time for exercise at the gym or on the yoga mat. Without doing those simple things, I would definitely have less energy and be a far less effective executive. Regardless of how you prefer to recharge and re-energize, you have to actually schedule time and do it. It's my observation that the people who are most stressed at work often are not recharging their batteries when they are away from the office.

Always be mentally checking in with yourself so that you're not on the edge of exhaustion—which doesn't serve anyone. Over the course of my career, I've become exceptionally good at balance and it's one of my company's core values. As a leader, I strive to be a great example of it. In the early days of a career, it's really hard to learn it while you're struggling and hustling. By being respected and appreciated by people around you for being balanced, it becomes easier to consistently model that behavior. As a cancer survivor, I believe that living fully in the present with daily gratitude for your job and simply being alive is most important. Attitude is everything—in business and in life! Worrying about the future which you cannot control causes most of the stress people experience. Let things that happen flow through you, observing them versus resisting them, and your life will become much fuller, simpler, and more rewarding.

KNOW HOW YOU (AND YOUR PEOPLE) OPERATE

There are a lot of different personality assessments and people prefer different ones; complete a few, and see if they're consistent with your self assessment. Your results may change at different stages in your life, so be aware of that. But some of it is your core wiring and how you naturally behave every day. Have your employees complete your favorite assessment tool too. Once you have the profiles of people on your team, you can adjust your leadership style to each person, taking into consideration their communication style and motivators. What is the most constructive way to handle communication at work? Different styles for different personality types may be the key.

Some popular personality assessments include DISC, Myers Briggs, and the Enneagram. All are good, but typically most impactful if the entire executive team around the table has completed their own assessment and they are shared with the team by an expert in a moderated session. As a stand-alone assessment they can also be interesting, but much less relevant since they all govern your relationships at work.

Importantly, these assessments should not be used independently for hiring decisions, since they simply govern communication styles and other aspects of a person in a team setting. There is no ideal personality profile, but it will give your boss and/or leadership team a lot of information about how to build a support and communication infrastructure around you so that you can thrive. As a CEO, I believe having assessments done on the team and then discussing them collectively is hugely important. It gives a team a common language to discuss their personality quirks while building camaraderie and a deeper understanding of your peers.

I recommend the DISC profile to organizations as a really simple yet impactful assessment to be used with executive teams. Typically, you can get it done for several hundred dollars and it takes approximately 15 minutes to complete. If you're having it done at work and you are a manager, I also recommend engaging a firm that specializes in the assessment to lead a team-building session to help you understand the team around you.

The very first letter in DISC is Dominance. The second one is I for Influence. Most CEOs are really high on the "D" scale, with a slightly lesser I. Or they have an equally high D and I, but typically very low levels of S and C—Steadiness and Compliance. When this is the case, it is ideal if the people around them have strong S and C levels to keep them on track with details and delivery of important items on time—this is often accomplished through the role of their assistant.

When you understand your team members' profiles, as well as your own, it really helps determine how you can work best together. You may also find that each team member may be better suited for a specific job based on their personality. For instance, salespeople score exceptionally high on the I scale, and often quite low on the C scale, which explains why many dislike using detailed tracking systems to record their calls. They are relationship people and are typically very "High I's," but dread the associated paperwork involved in tracking their daily activities.

There is no good or bad personality type, so you should not be afraid of any results you get. And don't let your personality type dictate the level you strive for. "What if I'm a strong SC and lower on the DI scale, but still aspire to become a CEO one day?" That's cool—be yourself and become a CEO. Just realize it may be a harder path for you as you try to develop certain characteristics you weren't naturally wired for.

The thing to remember is that if you are trying to adopt behaviors that are extremely outside of your comfort zone, this may place more stress on you in your workplace.

To consider an example that we often see in small, rapidly growing companies, consider the startup CEO. The truth is that company will likely have multiple different CEOs in the course of its life as a company. Just as executives go through different career stages, companies also have different stages that require different leadership strategies and personalities at the top. We are often hired by the board of a startup company to help transition the company from the technical founder CEO to a financially savvy, investor-focused CEO. Each has a different background, leadership profile, personality type, and will have a different style for communicating with and engaging their employees. The technical founder CEO builds the foundation and needs to be "hands on," focusing on the important details as well as the big picture, making an S and/or C perspective valuable. Then, the investor-focused CEO focuses on financing the company, launching products, and scaling revenue. They are more likely to have a high D and I score since they are more outward facing to engage the hearts and minds of employees, investors and customers as the company grows.

Again, just as you oriented yourself to your most satisfying career stage, you should also consider the stage of company you're best suited to lead—one where you'll be effective and enjoy the process. When you take that same CEO who loved the technology development and put them into the commercial stage of a company, they typically hate it. It's not their thing—they don't want to worry about driving revenue.

When I say there are two or three CEOs in the life of a company, most board members don't want to believe that—they really love to think that somebody founds a company and takes it all the way through its stages of development. But in reality that is quite unusual. A company matures through different stages and needs different leaders for each of those stages. That goes for the operating team of a company too. In a startup, you wear many hats and have a broad role, which is much less specialized. As companies develop, the function becomes laser focused and therefore companies seek expert help in that specific function.

Figuring out what you like to do and how you're naturally wired will help direct you towards the right stage of a company for you. Having self-awareness through the stages of your company's development is critical because you may be a rockstar and feel invincible at the early stage of a company and then, all of a sudden, things aren't as easy for you.

Usually in the early days of a company, the technology is dictating all of the choices and the marketing people have a really hard time getting their points across. This same conversation applies to startup people if they stay too long in the commercial stage. In my experience, if commercially-minded people join an early stage company too early, they're incredibly frustrated because they can't apply their skills and realize their passions in that company. And they may not even realize it about themselves.

I've had to take executives who have experienced a really bad outcome scenario and say, "What have you learned? What did you learn about the stage of the company? Do you agree that this was a development stage for the company? It was too early for someone of your talents."

Retrospectively, they finally figure it out. But it is hard to realize when you're in it. After all, you're one person living one career. Meanwhile, a search professional has seen it hundreds if not thousands of times: people choosing the wrong stage of company or the wrong place to apply themselves. And the stage of a company is another important factor to be thoughtful about when pursuing your perfect job.

It's actually painful to see executives who don't realize and accept this about themselves. Instead of embracing the corporate stage where they're best suited and what they enjoy the most, they move into the wrong stage and are later miserable. They seldom realize they should have left earlier, but everyone around them sees it. I recommend doing 360 degree reviews annually (even at your own request if not company mandated), to understand what your manager, peers, and direct reports think of your performance in your current role. Self-awareness of your current performance, coupled with your preference to career stage and company stage is the number one way to optimize your productivity and career achievements.

THE THREE STAGES OF A COMPANY

So what exactly are the stages of a company? It's helpful to think of them as similar to a person's career phases. But a person's career phase does not have to be the same as the company's stage. In fact, it's better if it isn't.

Startup Stage

A startup company is an emerging company that's still finding its footing.

The hallmark of a CEO who excels in a startup stage is innovation—light bulbs are going off over their head all the time. They are typically entrepreneurial, highly committed, and fearless on every level. They are highly risk tolerant and go forward because they feel it is their calling. They tend to identify their employees through their personal network because they are proven, and it also helps to conserve cash versus engaging a search firm.

Seasoned entrepreneurial founders know exactly when to hand off a company. An experienced entrepreneur that realizes his strengths and passion are in leading startups will hand the company to a new leader very gracefully, then go and create a new business. The worst thing a startup CEO can do is hold onto an organization or business for too long and micromanage everything. They often hire great people, but they won't let them do their jobs—you don't want to be that person. If you are the inventor, an entrepreneurial spirit, know your strengths and be the one who graciously bows out at the right time. You can continue to be a stakeholder in that company, but it's best to transition it to a commercially-minded CEO as soon as practical so that the company can thrive.

Commercial Stage

The commercial stage is where the company is becoming visible within the marketplace it serves.

Commercial stage companies are skilled at product definition and launch. Once launched, they become very sales-driven. And so are their CEOs, who typically must have prior sales and marketing leadership experience. Without strong financial and commercialization skills, you need not apply.

The typical commercial stage CEO has an engaging personality and good deal-making and/or partnering abilities. The founder CEO of the startup was very technical or innovative—they discovered something that was really fascinating or novel. This CEO will sell that product or service, and ensure the world knows about it. Commercial stage CEOs can tell a really good story to investors and raise money to finance the company, which is one of the most important features at this stage. Consistent internal and external communications and messaging to employees and investors is critical.

I often say a CEO has 3 roles: (1) to finance the company (2) hire great employees and (3) inspire the employees to deliver upon the company's mission and vision. Recently, I was at a CEO conference in Napa with a mix of early stage and commercial stage companies and CEOs. The hardest thing for the transitioning start-up to commercial stage CEO was letting go of the notion that as CEO they should do it all. At this stage, you can't. To reiterate, as a CEO, your job at the commercial stage is to focus on three things: raising money, hiring people, and inspiring people.

And that's a very different thing than being a startup CEO. A lot of people want to continue to be the entrepreneurial CEO, hands on and in the weeds, but if that style is your passion, you will have to leave each company when it gets too mature and seek out your next startup.

There's a very clear demarcation in businesses between the commercial stage and non-commercial stage companies. Without a product on the market, entirely different skill sets are needed. And the minute you start launching products, it becomes an entirely different company. It goes from research and development (R & D)-driven to sales and marketing-driven, which is quite an adjustment for an organization. The CEO must help affect this change and be sure R & D is not still calling all the shots when sales, marketing, and their customers should be instead. I once led commercial operations for a startup that made this transition and it was quite difficult to achieve that handoff, which in the end was necessary. During this stage, the successful CEO will need to work on changing the power center from R&D to sales, while maintaining the spirit of the technical team who got them this far.

Globalization Stage

Lastly, there's the globalization stage when the company is participating in the international markets.

Is there any distinction from commercialization to a global expansion? In some instances, if you're a commercially experienced executive, you will have enough global knowledge and ability to move into being a multinational leader with no problem. The key here is global experience and knowing how to work on a global scale and manage thousands of people. Globalization often requires a very different leader, particularly if the prior CEO didn't have multi-national experience.

Compensation also changes as you progress through the stages of CEO. The entrepreneurial CEO is willing to trade cash for equity every time. Their goal is to have a big win after working long, hard hours and shouldering a lot of financial risk while doing so. Commercial stage CEOs typically earn a bit more cash and less equity, and if they're smart are still willing to trade some cash for equity. When a person becomes a multinational CEO, they are compensated with higher cash and less options, but instead long term incentive bonuses are the norm. The progression typically goes like this: the startup CEO takes less cash for more equity, the middle commercial CEO takes an even slice of cash and equity, and the global CEO gets a generous salary with a sizable bonus of long-term, monetary incentive every year. The package changes—and that's why they have the big cash for those CEOs. They didn't take as much risk and help create the company, so there is less upside when the options pay out with the big win.

Your sensitivity around risk, if you're willing to take it or not, also helps shape what level of company suits you best. If you're the entrepreneurial founder-type with nothing to lose, you should start a company. But some of us aren't that way and aren't willing to trade cash for equity. If this is you, don't waste your time pursuing an early stage company role because they're going to ask you to trade your cash for equity and you're not comfortable with that degree of risk. As a company matures, the compensation structure will change, but if you prefer and desire one specific type of compensation, make sure you're entering the right stage of company.

THE DARK SIDE OF DRIVE

In the earlier chapter on Mindset, we talked about drive and the positives it can bring in terms of motivation and happiness. Most female executives who are incredibly driven have experienced the dark side of drive, however. Personally, I've struggled with the dark side for years. The dark side of drive is when you work yourself into the ground, feel under appreciated, and continue that cycle. It's a recipe for disaster, and in your early days, it's an easy trap to fall into as you're working to build value. But the end result—if not addressed—is burnout.

Burnout leads to exhaustion and an eventual meltdown of your psyche. It's easy to give up on your career when you don't feel you are good enough and think you need to work longer, harder hours to be noticed as a worthy employee. But that's a ridiculous mindset and can be difficult to overcome. You need to know that if you are committed to your career and doing your best to learn and grow that you are absolutely good enough.

I believe many female executives lack confidence which causes this behavior, and we try to build confidence through exhibiting excellence on the job. Instead, we should build confidence through planning and fearless execution against our career development plan. I've observed women overworking both at the office and then at home trying hard to be noticed. In my experience, that isn't how you get noticed in the workplace though—that's how you get put in a corner and told, *"Wow, you're really good at doing that. You should keep doing it!"* It's a self-destructive way to handle your career that only leads to feelings of inadequacy when your hard work isn't rewarded.

Once you realize your drive is controlling you, it's time to change that pattern and instead respect and appreciate yourself. As I mentioned earlier, I coach all female executives that they should be spending 25 percent of their time on themselves and 75 percent on their employer, which in my experience is more often how men tend to conduct their careers. You deserve to have an outstanding career—and that needs to be a core belief. Work on your self-esteem and develop the confidence to get yourself to believe that point. Observe the majority of male executives around you who have this mindset and behave accordingly—they're not overworking themselves or trying to be noticed, but rather living by their internal compass and naturally showing up with confidence.

SPIN YOUR DRIVE POSITIVELY

Instead of letting your drive control you, control your drive by channeling that energy into developing yourself. Schedule your 25% time to read books, see coaches, meet mentors and recruiters, network, and really care about your own career—both personally and professionally. Get yourself on track and then stop trying to get noticed at work in the quest for perfection on the job.

The alternative to overworking is to strategize and determine where you can add value. Schedule a constructive dialogue with your CEO or your manager about areas for improvement and where you think you could make a big difference. When you pitch your ideas to your superiors, say, "I've been observing everything that's going on around here and I really think I could make a difference to the company and in parallel realize a career development opportunity. I propose we..." And then explain your thoughts and how your idea would benefit the company.

Don't do a career death spiral by overworking yourself to try to get noticed. Work smarter, not harder, and deal directly with your superiors, pitching ideas to improve their lives while adding value and advancing your career. This is how a conscious executive controls their career. At the same time, know that you have a dark side and have to schedule time for relaxation, your family, and exercise to stay balanced.

Allocate your time properly and avoid spreading yourself too thin. Remember, as Abraham Lincoln once said, "If I had eight hours to chop down a tree, I'd spend six sharpening my ax." Don't just blindly hack at a problem, take your time, think things through, and sharpen your ax.

I see so many women in the workplace who want to be considered irreplaceable, but shoot themselves in the foot by doing this. They do a job exceptionally well and then don't speak up about what they want to do next. What they should be thinking about is where they're going, who will be their successor, and how to develop that successor.

They need to think about their next career conversation and how to add more value to the company in a way that gives them more leverage for that conversation. Your boss will be more receptive to moving you into a new role if you have developed a person to fill your role instead of making yourself irreplaceable. These women wrongly think hoarding knowledge will make them powerful and valuable when it really makes them stagnant and stuck.

THE MARRIAGE OF PERSONAL AND PROFESSIONAL

This all returns to self-care. Synchronize your personal and your professional lives because they are intertwined. I've seen many, many executives who are super-powered in the workplace and miserable at home. Obviously, this isn't the right equation for anyone. It detracts from your ability to be a high-powered executive. You may think you have it all together, but you really don't. It can be the other way around too—that the family life is rocking and rolling and the career is really struggling. A fully-formed executive has to have all channels operating smoothly. The greatest risk to female professional executives is not honoring the fact that you have to invest in both. You have to build relationships in the workplace and at home. These people are all equally important to your success and survival as an executive.

Planning for your personal life doesn't need to be a separate exercise; in fact, it shouldn't be, because both your work and personal life are integrated into your whole self—mind, body, and spirit.

Case in point, when I was a member in the CEO development organization Vistage, during our monthly meetings we routinely intertwined both personal and professional aspects of leadership all the time, both in a group setting and in one-on-one coaching sessions. Within the group, my peer CEOs' family issues were raised and solved with nearly equal frequency and completely equal intensity. Whether it's a work issue or a home issue, we're trying to help each other navigate our career challenges, which included both personal and professional. We were aware that without harmony on all fronts, we can't be happy and successful.

When you set a goal or aspiration for your work life, can you accommodate your family and your health while maintaining your work-driven mindset? That's an important question you need to ask yourself.

If you have a family, you need to make sure that they're well taken care of, but it doesn't mean that it has to be you managing the home at every minute. A partnership with your spouse involves negotiation on a consistent basis. You need to constantly ask each other: *"Is it still working for us? What should we change?"* Have a meeting with each other at least quarterly to figure out who's making the compromises and how your home responsibilities are best balanced, which will change as you move through your careers.

The question in a dual-income household becomes, "Which one of us should step away from their career to focus on the home?" Often, the decision is made in favor of the highest earner—but not always. And it doesn't always have to be the woman stepping away from her career, either. It is very common to see successful female executives whose spouses cover the at-home duties, and they tell us they couldn't have advanced as far and fast without that assistance. Executive men have had this luxury for years, and many smart, successful women have now enjoyed the same.

You will make some compromises. Your partner will make some compromises. You can also take turns compromising so no one becomes resentful. I talked to a female chief operating officer whose husband had followed her throughout all of these executive roles. Now they're in a place where he gets to realize his goals and they can both have enjoyable careers. Be very cognizant that your spouse is making this commitment to you and that you're a team raising your children or taking care of the home. The happiest professional women I have known have a fair and balanced partnership with their spouse. If you can't strike that balance, it's going to be very difficult for you as a mother, a spouse, and an executive to have happiness and success. The challenges of the personal bleed into the professional at some point.

If you do choose to step away from your career while you're running your household, you haven't really stepped away—you're now simply the CEO of a different organization. If you have that CEO mentality and that's your aspiration, really view yourself as the CEO of the household or CEO of your life during this time period: the business side, the personal, all departments and divisions. Count it as the year(s) you decided to be CEO of the household and practice those same CEO skills you use in the workplace to keep your skills sharp and your confidence in tact.

For a female executive who is running both sides of her life as the CEO, she and her spouse should agree to be co-CEOs at home. You can have employees in that partnership, such as people who help you with the children, the cleaning, or the cooking. I'm a huge advocate of spending your weekends together but not cleaning the house or doing mundane things. Your time is worth way more than that. Figure out a way to get some assistance, especially if you're on the executive track, to help you spend quality time with your spouse and your family.

Every time you change employers, you have the opportunity to recreate yourself and establish boundaries again. Never give up your family life for the sake of an employer. Your current employer may not respect your boundaries, but you can always start fresh with a new employer and set up a new flexibility agreement from the start. Upon interviewing, talk about the things you need that are important for you to live a happy, balanced life. People really respect an executive that values having a couple of hours in the evening with their family. Set boundaries. Say, *"I am completely open to taking calls and meetings at any time except from 6 to 8 p.m. because I have dinner with my family and then read my children bedtime stories. Afterwards, I'll be available."*

Every single successful executive I know sets these boundaries. If your employer doesn't respect your commitment to your family or your health, then they're not the right organization to work for. For awhile, I worked for Roche, a European company that really values long summer holidays and family time. They have long maternity leaves and are much more balanced than we are here in the U.S. Find an organization that has core values you agree with and you'll be much better served. When you set necessary boundaries for yourself, they will respect them, too. Carve out the time to take care of yourself through exercise and personal planning marked in your calendar. If you have an assistant, tell your assistant these are the times you're not available. Treat those times as sacred. An employer can't take advantage of you if you establish boundaries from the start.

What I have learned from a number of executive women, myself included, is that if you're a Driver in the DISC profile, you are best surrounded by people who do the things that you don't do as well. In a DISC profile, that's support and compliance—examples are taking the kids to school every day on time or doing the grocery shopping. People are compatible with you because the two of you aren't the same and you should value that. Sit down and talk it through so you and your partner have clearly defined roles. Your partner's job needs to be important and you need to give them the ability to make all of the decisions around this job. If he's also a high powered Driver executive and/or simply not the supportive type, you may want to hire a personal assistant or a nanny to help with the children, finances permitting.

Now that you're an executive woman, you're smart enough to know that if you had an employee working with you, they would have their own specific job and you would not interfere. Don't micromanage your spouse or do all the work for the partnership. Once you have negotiated and agreed upon your mutual roles, your spouse needs to feel valued, important, and be treated as a contributor. I've seen a lot of marriages melt down because the partner didn't feel like they had a really important or equal job, and/or they didn't feel appreciated. This is a serious consideration for executive women and one often overlooked in the quest for success. Please take good care to include your personal life in your annual planning process, since neglecting your home life is a sure path to unintended negative consequences.

ACTION ITEMS:

- **Avoid indecisiveness:** Be bold, decisive, and efficient when approaching a career challenge or important decision.

- **Be solutions-focused:** Propose your top three options and recommended solutions to your manager rather than simply presenting the problem.

- **Schedule self-care:** Put time on your calendar to refresh yourself to avoid burn-out.

- **Learn your best communication style:** Complete one or more personality assessments, and have the results translated by an experienced career coach.

- **Evaluate your company stage:** Determine whether it is appropriate for your current career development aspirations.

- **Channel your drive:** Find value creation opportunities at your current employer, and pitch them to your manager.

- **Synchronize personal and professional:** Review your Career Map and annual plans with your partner quarterly.

WE ARE NOT MINI-MEN

OVERCOMING THE MYTH OF THE FEMALE EXECUTIVE

People like to characterize successful female executives as evil, malicious employees who don't support each other. But in my entire career, I have never seen this. Because this misperception of female executives exists, the struggle becomes actually overcoming the negative bias. Both men and women today are afraid that's how we're going to show up and behave on the job. I recently hired a President to work as my right hand guy, and as he considered the opportunity he very thoughtfully said, "I've never worked for a female CEO before." And I wondered, "Is there a difference between male and female CEOs? Honestly, what does that even mean? Are you afraid that I'm going to turn on you?"

THE NEW GENERATION OF FEMALE LEADERS

The original powerful women (think Margaret Thatcher) were ironclad and felt they had to show up like men to be taken seriously. Now we have a "new generation" of female executives who are more powerful when they own all the dimensions of themselves.

But I've learned the number one thing that male board members and CEOs worry about with female executives is women crying in meetings—they still tell me this. On several occasions, we've needed to replace a female CEO because, amongst other issues, she was judged to be too emotionally unstable due to emotional outbursts ending with crying in board meetings.

Being too emotional at work is a negative thing for anyone, regardless of gender. Executive experience tells me you shouldn't get mad at work. You should not express that level of emotion or intensity even if you feel it. Control yourself because it's a business transaction, all in the name of business. If you've pre-thought your position and you're coming in with balanced suggestions, you shouldn't be getting that distressed.

Vulnerability is an exceptional quality in men and women alike—I believe they both have to be vulnerable in the workplace to be true leaders. It is an executive strength to express your passion and emotion without crying. Learning to do that is really important: be vulnerable, be transparent, say how you really feel—just please don't cry at work, unless you're in a private office setting with a colleague you trust to keep your feelings in confidence.

I'll use my team's celebration for my birthday as an example. I was so emotional, but I always remember that when you cry, it makes everyone uncomfortable. It particularly makes men uncomfortable because they don't know how to deal with it. If you think about the male executive's mind, they often think they need to solve the cause of the tears. Alienating your coworkers and partners is a very ineffective way to lead. Learn to express emotion and vulnerability in front of everyone without crying.

AMN Healthcare's CEO Susan Salka is a great example of a vulnerable and powerful woman. If you ever have the opportunity to see Susan Salka speak, do it—she's remarkable. She's been with AMN for thirty years and loves her team more than you could imagine. She exhibits sincere gratitude and thankfulness on the stage, but without uncomfortable emotion. Too much emotion for the positive or negative can be misconstrued. One of the greatest things that leaders can do is control their presence at all times. Your team gets a lot of confidence from the way you show up and present yourself. Practice delivering your message with a positive spin that is controlled but not artificial. It will make your entire organization more confident.

With that said, we do have to own our femininity and not aim to be stoic female versions of our masculine counterparts. And that includes dressing like women. Professional, yet decidedly female—we should not feel like we have to be mini-men and wear the same clothes they wear. When women actually show up as women with incredible competence and confidence in their appearance, it's a game changer. Don't be overly sexy or over the top—stick to professional wear and remember that today "professional" does not equal "manly."

Once, a female CEO confided to me that she has a huge preponderance of female executives on her team, almost unbalanced in their numbers. It feels awkward, but this reversal is actually what we deal with every day—a male majority in business. Then, that female CEO confessed she actually loves the balance around the table because women will debate incessantly about all of the possibilities whereas men tend to just slice through the deliberation and make a decision. Different communication styles yield different results and allow different types of processing to happen. In fact, it is ideal to have diversity of thought and options around the table. It's been proven in many studies that executive team diversity makes companies more innovative, and companies with female CEOs exhibit better financial performance.

That's why the myth of the female executive makes me crazy. If you listen to old-school thinking, a lot of people believe we are only successful if we're these stereotypical mini-men wearing business suits. The earmark of the executive female myth is that we're super decisive, almost to a fault, and that we behave as mean, angry individuals in the workplace to show our competence and success. Couple that with many female executives' beliefs that all other women out there are competing with and holding them back, and you have a perpetuated myth of the classic angry-female-executive-in-the-boardroom.

Where did this myth of the female executive come from? I think that, to some extent, men are threatened by women in the workplace—they've historically owned it. Movies don't help. They capitalize upon the trope of the bitch in the boardroom or the overbearing female executive. *The Devil Wears Prada* is a classic movie example that comes to mind.

The entertainment industry tends to show the kind of mean-spirited boss lady—where she is raging and angry at life. There's a rare woman like that, for sure, but there are also a lot of men in that same vein. The fact that media stereotypes female executives this way is fascinating to me—the majority of successful female executives I've seen are really balanced, thoughtful team players who develop people and collaborators.

Meanwhile, on television, there's never been a stronger female leader than Oprah. She recreated what it means to be a female executive in the public eye. And she did so with class, confidence, and ability far beyond her formal training. She went from anchorwoman to billionaire with a brand that supports female empowerment. She's proof that the female executive myth is, in fact, a myth.

Even as far back as the cavemen days, women have historically been very good at certain things like empathetic caretaking, team development, and collaboration. Everything the female executive myth tries to say we don't do. Men are traditionally good at decisiveness and taking quick action. The perfect executive has all of these competencies and exhibits all of the ideal aspects of leadership. At the end of the day, the fully formed executive—regardless of gender—is exceptional at developing and inspiring people, including themselves.

This teamwork, collaboration, and leadership competency women have is grounded in multitasking. So if we look at the way women behave in the world today, most of us are such extreme multitaskers—it's almost unbelievable and unsustainable how good we are at it. As a result, we can be on many teams, we can lead many processes, and we can develop a lot of people at once. Our human nature makes us exceptionally good at all of it just by practice and performance. I have not met this internally focused, out-for-herself myth executive yet and those misconceptions are infuriating.

Back when I was first becoming an executive, women did try to dress and behave like men in order to be honored in the boardroom or in conversation. Emulating how men approached business was the only model we had. As time progressed over the past twenty to twenty-five years, women started owning their femininity and showing up wearing and doing what made them feel comfortable. They were being professional, polished and female—a much more effective route, in my opinion, to success. If you are an incredible, approachable human who happens to be female while you're at the boardroom table, I think everyone is happier to work with you. You're not putting on some sort of a show of trying to be someone other than who you are. Being your authentic self is paramount in the workplace.

NORMS ARE NORMAL BUT AUTHENTIC ISN'T AVERAGE

Now I can't even imagine being someone else, but it's taken me awhile to evolve to this place. Again, in my early sales days, it was a case of "let's all behave the same way." We all wore the same suits and were driven by the same goals. It's not a great feeling, and nobody wants to deal with a lack of authenticity or any behavior other than what is natural to you. Trying to act like someone you're not will put you under a lot of stress in the workplace.

It comes down to owning yourself and being who you are now. Of course, there are certain limitations—if you have tattoos all over your body or wear all leather on the weekends, you would want to dress appropriately for and in the workplace so that you'll be treated as the executive you aspire to be. There are certain normal standards of business attire that you need to honor, but your workplace will let you know which ones matter to them. If you want an executive team to respect you, you'll have to respect its sensibilities.

One of the things we've started doing for candidates we're sending to interviews is to ask the company what's appropriate attire for their workplace. If a candidate shows up in a suit and tie while the entire company is wearing golf shirts, it's really uncomfortable for everybody. The norms have changed so much that as executive recruiters, we have to ask in advance what the candidate should wear. We don't want anyone to feel out of place and we don't want the people interviewing them to get the wrong impression of the person (for instance being judged as being too formal for the environment if they show up in a full business suit). Adjust your attire to whatever workplace you've adopted and don't go too far outside the cultural norms. If you don't feel comfortable strictly within in the norms, branch out a bit, but do so respectfully and gradually.

I've evolved to a place where I wear dresses and skirts nearly every single day. I find them comfortable and I feel feminine. I'm just who I am and colors are a part of that—I wear a lot of bright colors which make me feel more confident. You have to channel a professional form of your true, authentic self. There was a lot of time in my career where I would wear pants every day—I put on the matching, professional business suits just like everyone else. Thankfully, today norms have changed and people wear more separates and comfortable clothes at work while still being professional—nothing too risqué, nothing too matronly. Both of those extremes get misinterpreted in a workplace and will for the foreseeable future.

There is a fine line—some women think that showing some cleavage is honoring their femininity, but you have to be careful about that. If it's a work or professional event, be professional at all times, and low-cut shirts and too-short skirts are still out of the norm. Be professional and polished, even after work. Open-toed shoes are also still on the edge depending on where you live. It's taken me a long time, but as a California native in the summer I have now opted to go to open-toed shoes on days when I'm in the office, which is acceptable in our market. However, if I'm seeing customers, I'm still very thoughtful about that. Think about what would be appropriate in their workplace. A lot of places I go have labs or clean rooms, and for touring them close-toed shoes are a must. Be practical about your wardrobe choices for the type of work environments you frequent.

When I'm going to meet with customers, I have to think about their workplace cultures. You can tell a lot from a company's website. For instance, if their cover photo is a bunch of middle-aged white guys wearing suits and ties, take that into account. For instance, I work with a company in Boston with portraits of their employees and all of their employees' dogs on their executive site. The dogs wear bow ties and little vests and are mixed in with the employees. It's the craziest, cutest thing I've ever seen. And by looking at that website, you can tell that company is very relaxed and very fun. It's a casual environment, with young energized executives with their dogs in the workplace.

If you know the company and how they conduct themselves, dress accordingly. Don't be too loud if you know they're conservative and vice versa. Don't be too clean-cut if you know they're artsy. And if the company's sensibility is vastly different from your own, take that into consideration when deciding to work there. Remember, your choices and how you present yourself as you walk into a room say so much about you. Get judged as the corporate executive that you are and avoid distracting from your value with your clothing. You want to exude the statement, "You don't ever need to pay attention to what I'm wearing because it's so appropriate."

Boardroom wardrobe is more conservative. On days you know you have a board meeting, you might dress differently than you dress the rest of week. At the executive level, the old-school attitudes about dress still persist in some circles. Know who you might be spending time with and their attitudes toward business attire—it may differ from your everyday crowd. Don't go too far too fast, and pay attention to your workplace and coworkers. Carefully select your clothing to go with the events and occasions of that particular day.

In addition, pay attention to the executive women in your new workplace. They are women who have succeeded in the environment you're moving into. Instead of trying to be the only woman in the boardroom, ideally select companies that are female-friendly with women in positions of authority. This is a good starting place—they've already cultivated an environment that embraces female executives like you. Female-friendly corporations used to not exist, and women had to show up to uncomfortable or even hostile workplaces without any representation. Times have changed, and you shouldn't have to put yourself through that anymore. So choose your next employer wisely, and make sure you don't have to.

OWNING YOUR FEMININE POWER

The JP Morgan Healthcare Conference is a big event where bankers and investors all gather in San Francisco. They're mostly men in gray suits with ties standing in a forum trying to talk to each other. And then, in the middle of all of them, there will be one spectacular woman in an amazing colored outfit. Embrace being the outlier—stand out and be different. Our difference is our advantage.

Be who you are and be proud of it. Do not ever feel compromised because you're a woman—in my professional opinion and based on my experience, it's actually an advantage. Come into every situation with the mindset of feminine pride. Be careful about being an ardent feminist at work or favoring women all of the time, but it's natural to feel comfortable in your body as a woman. Just be proud to be a woman in the workplace and ideally involve yourself with organizations that support and advance women.

I currently am on the boards of and support women's leadership programs and multiple women's health non-profits (breast and ovarian cancer), to lead by example and personally make a contribution and a difference to things that affect women. My personal objective is advancing all causes that empower women for the next ten years, and I make my non-profit contributions of time and money accordingly. Get involved with whatever speaks to you.

These things are all key to being proud to be a woman. I can't even imagine operating any other way, and the female executives I know feel the same. Especially the higher up the ranks you go. Even today, only three percent of CEOs in the U.S. are female when it should be closer to half. We need more female executives coming forward with confidence and pride instead of feeling discriminated against and alienated.

But to really start owning your own feminine power is an achievement that takes a lifetime. And I applaud you if you're young and already feeling it, but it takes a while to really come into your own and feel incredibly empowered. I have always known that people can do insurmountable feats just by digging deeper into themselves—the sky's the limit on what humans can accomplish. We just need to put in the work to find our sweet spot.

Self-actualization comes from operating in that sweet spot. Have a vision you're really inspired by that you're working towards. And, no matter where you are, even if you're working in a place that doesn't honor your long term objectives, know why you're there. Show up knowing it is adding value to who you are and part of your executive career path. Show up with confidence and be your best self every day. Your positive attitude will have a much greater impact than just being excellent at your job.

For forty hours every week, you interact with internal and external customers. And both deserve to see the human side of you. Your internal customers are the people working with you—your team. Then there are the external or outward customers your team sells a product or service to. If you only care about forward or outward facing customer interactions and mistreat your internal customers by undermining your humanity, you've totally missed the boat. The people around you will in fact make or break your career every single time. If you show up with an abundance of happiness and give out joy, your team or internal customers will deliver for you—everyone is willing to help each other and that's a sure recipe for success. Own your feminine power and use it to bolster your team as well as your external customers—success starts from the inside and goes out.

Being feminine in the workplace means being comfortable being yourself, and it directly affects your attitude. If you always give your good, natural energy to people, you don't have to have a different work persona that's inauthentic. As an example, an accomplished executive woman I know constantly worries about being perfect and puts on an uncomfortable veneer at work. She strives for constant, idealized professionalism instead of just being her fun, wonderful, joyful self—the one I see when we're not in the workplace. She would be so much more effective if she could bring her wonderful, authentic self to her job, all day every day. When you let down your guard, stop trying to be perfect all the time, and just be human, that's a powerful thing.

AUTHENTICITY WITHOUT OVERSHARING

When talking about authenticity, there is a line and it makes people uncomfortable when you cross it and enter into oversharing.

Sharing too much personal information in the workplace, on any level, is inappropriate. Oversharing personal information in the workplace is not required and definitely not appreciated. It isn't what the job is about. A woman may feel like she's doing the company and the leadership team a favor by letting them know what's going on in her personal life or her personal future plans, but she shouldn't even go there. Your whole personal circumstance can change complete-ly—that's life. Don't share an unnecessary hypothetical.

Limit talk of your personal life to times when you're in a party setting or on a break, and even then keep it casual. It's not good to bring up those types of things all day long. It can make people uncomfortable and make some think you're not focused. Everyone around you should know you revere your children and family. As I said before, the best executives I know are balanced and the best companies value familial relationships, but those relationships don't have to be a consistent topic of conversation in your workplace.

You'll discern on a person-by-person basis whether they need to talk about their families or children. Be cognizant and thoughtful about that, but of course feel free to have pictures of your kids all over your office—that's your space. Just be conscientious of other people's spaces.

Having boundaries is a normal part of work life. Just as you should turn off your phone and be completely with your family while you're on vacation or after work hours, try not to bring any at-home issues into the workplace. Everyone should know that you are com-mitted to your family as much as you're committed to your job, but that also goes in reverse and for others. Respect their boundaries and personal lives.

An important distinction I want everyone to realize is that own-ing your feminine power is not oversharing or making others feel uncomfortable under the guise of equality. That being said, there are some uniquely female situations in the workplace that must be addressed.

HOW TO APPROACH MATERNITY LEAVE

First of all, discrimination based upon pregnancy is illegal. If necessary, women need to reiterate to their employers that men have children all of the time and it isn't an issue. Women marry and have children—it's going to happen. Plan out your maternity leave ahead of time with your employer and everyone will feel secure knowing how it will work. It's the same as resigning—someone will be filling in when you're out of the office and you'll prepare them for the task before you go.

When interviewing, the best way to handle the potential of pregnancy is to treat the possibility as a non-issue. They won't be asking about it and you shouldn't bring it up when they ask about your goals for the next three to five years. Those goals may include having a child, but that's obviously a personal goal, not a professional one. Why would you even bring it up? It's not important or necessary to the topic at hand. You'd be compromised if you decided to volunteer that information because you'd be oversharing instead of owning your feminine power.

A female CEO told me she went on a road show when she was nine months pregnant. She was trying to raise money for her company, but all of the Venture Capitalists were scared to put money into her business—they knew and they even told her they had concerns that her pregnancy would sideline her for a bit. She was infuriated—they never would have mentioned that to a man whose wife was expecting to deliver a baby within the next month. And, of course, as a female CEO she had her maternity leave all planned out and her great executive team taking care of the company for her few months of planned leave.

Similarly, I have a female board member who just had twins and she was off for two or three months. When she returned, she just parachuted in and was back at the table doing everything she would otherwise do. During those two to three months, the process went on without her and she integrated back in seamlessly.

This goes back to not working yourself into a corner. Don't make your employer think you are irreplaceable—always be grooming a replacement either as an exit strategy for promotion or for taking planned medical leave. You should be able to take a couple of months off to have a child. If not, you're either in the wrong place or have made yourself irreplaceable, which is also a negative thing.

One of the top skills of an executive is to make sure you have a good succession plan. You want to be able to keep moving in your career. One of your jobs is to make sure the people around you are strong enough to carry on your job without you around. People who hoard information and knowledge are limiting their executive development. Your team and systems should be so strong that nobody should miss a beat if you're going to be away for two months. Plan well and everyone will know how it's going to be managed. The company will survive your absence.

ACTION ITEMS:

- **Control your Emotions:** Approach business challenges with a professional, solutions-oriented presentation.

- **Practice vulnerability:** Learn to express your compassion and feelings without tears.

- **Own your feminine power:** Dress appropriately yet professionally female—be yourself!

- **Express your natural strengths:** Emphasize your uniquely feminine approach to empathetic leadership, team development, collaboration, etc.

- **Reject perfection:** Strive for authenticity.

- **Enforce boundaries:** Avoid oversharing personal information in the workplace.

- **Plan your leave:** Approach maternity leave by presenting a thoughtful plan for your employer.

THE CAREER PATH PROCESS

At this stage, you're well along your career path. You probably have a secure position as a mid-level executive. You may even be on your way towards becoming a CEO if that's your aspiration. But your current position shouldn't make you complacent—finding and pursuing your passion place takes a lifetime and you should always be growing and learning.

The later part of your career process is more circular than the previous linear progression of steps. All of these pieces are things you should be revisiting and maintaining. Nothing takes precedence over another, but they all center around one main concept: doing your homework.

DO YOUR HOMEWORK

Whenever you're looking for new career opportunities, whether it's a lateral move in an industry you already know or a return to the emerging career stage in a new field, do some research. Start by reading every book you can about the industry and go through the same steps I outlined earlier: evaluate five to ten companies you'd like to work for, then find a way to speak with people who work at the companies that best align with your goals and sensibilities.

Identify people that are working in your desired career and shadow them. Learn from them and ask them to mentor you. Mentors and shadowing prepare you for a job interview better than going in with only having read of the role's duties. You'll feel confident you know what the job is actually about.

You may not be changing companies or fields at all. Maybe you're trying to sell a new product. Again, do your homework, both on the product you're presenting and the company you're presenting it to. If you have wicked product knowledge, you can pretty much walk in and deliver a pitch to anybody because it's not about you—it's about the product.

BUILD AND MAINTAIN YOUR NETWORK

You can't just stumble into a great network—you have to go out of your way to build it. Remember, people have gone to jail for taking client lists. But social networks are another animal entirely.

Each of our social networks existed before and after we came into any of our jobs. Because of executive search, my LinkedIn network is currently over fifteen thousand people—I can't give it back. It will exist and will follow me no matter who I work for. Because of this, it is in your best interest to build your social network on your own. That is something that travels with you and you can leverage in the future.

Once, I hired a search professional whose former employer did try to suggest she wasn't allowed to talk to her LinkedIn network. The employer was also a search professional and the whole affair was very unusual and, of course, not legally enforceable. Social networks are not the same as client lists.

LinkedIn

LinkedIn is an incredible tool. I hope it will remain more or less a free network to its users. Essentially, it's a living resume. Spend time making it represent your most employable and marketable self. This is the place that potential employers look all day long. List all of your board affiliations, all of your achievements, awards, professional interests, and everything noteworthy—your entire profile should be really sharp.

From a search perspective, if we find that someone's not on LinkedIn (which is highly unusual), you simply will not get called for jobs. It's used around the world by executive search firms, staffing firms, and employers. It's the first place people look when they need great people for great jobs. Make your profile both detailed and differentiated.

As beneficial as LinkedIn can be, things like Facebook and Instagram can be very detrimental. Anything you've ever posted is still alive and can be found. That's a scary statement. I've seen very negative ramifications to candidates based upon seemingly innocuous postings on social media—take great care to ensure you don't become one of those statistics. As an executive woman, I really limit my participation on Facebook from a personal perspective and stick to networking on LinkedIn. I'm very cautious about what I endorse on Linkedin, stay apolitical and middle of the road there.

Networking

Networking is probably the single greatest reason for my success. But I didn't actually realize I was building a network while I was doing it. I left each company on good terms and therefore took each network of positive working relationships with me. At each subsequent job, I developed a bigger and bigger network. Then I came into search, not realizing I actually had a really substantial network because of my job history and the good relationships I had built along the way. I had never thought of myself as a big networker, but I never burned bridges and I always prided myself on keeping positive working relationships even upon exit.

While later building a business in San Diego, I originally made a concerted effort to stay within my life sciences vertical. I actually thought in the early days of building my business, "Why would I need to know anyone else?" And then I joined several nonprofit boards that were cross-sectional to all industries and built a much more broad network, comprised of business leaders across all sectors. Now, I feel like I know most of the key players in the city, and have resource people in every sector. And I've subsequently come to believe that your network is actually everything! To create a career of substance and to be locally recognized, you need to develop a cross-industry network.

When you get to the highest levels and you want to be on boards, it all happens through the network. Still today, unfortunately seventy percent of board searches are filled through the board's network and therefore don't go through a search firm, even within public companies. So when you tell me—after you've been a great, successful executive—that you want to serve on a board, I'll tell you that you should in fact focus most of your efforts on your personal network. Don't simply ask search professionals for help—there is a high likelihood it's going to happen through your network and through your personal efforts.

But for all other roles, it is also imperative to know all the executive search professionals that work in your industry sector—we're a very critical part of the network and involved in the majority of VP and C-level roles. I'm not sure people even realize that—men understand this network and call us all day long. Strangely, I don't get women calling me to network very often. It's unfortunate, because I know women are instead spending their time overworking and overachieving in these industries and likely feel they're too busy to make the calls. Men are advancing their own careers by being very strategic and thoughtful about building their personal networks. I advise women do the same.

ACTION ITEMS:

- **Do your Homework:** Research career opportunities thoroughly, including interviewing people currently in the roles.

- **Develop your Network:** Meet and include at least three "industry-specific" executive search professionals in your network.

- **Keep in Touch:** Attend local networking events and schedule dedicated time with key influencers in your network.

- **Leverage Social Media:** Carefully control the content your post, realizing it is your "online resume."

INTERVIEW TO WIN

*The only person you are destined to become
is the person you decide to be.*

Ralph Waldo Emerson

By this time, you shouldn't be a stranger to interviews, but that doesn't mean you can't become expert at them. Interviews are where preparation meets opportunity. It goes back to doing your home-work—research each company before you go in to meet with their leadership team. Do they share your values online? Are they on your path to your big North Star goal?

TAKE THE CALL

Recruiters will call you. You'll need to know your parameters in advance: What are you willing to entertain? What's your perfect fit and ideal next role? If it doesn't meet your minimum criteria then don't spend a lot of time on it—instead just give them a referral.

Take the call, talk to the person, see if you can help them and, if you can help them, refer them forward. If you don't shut the door on them, that recruiter becomes part of your network and they'll keep calling you. Eventually, they could have something of interest for you personally, which could lead to your next career opportunity.

INTERVIEW THE HIRING MANAGER(S) ABOUT THEIR LEADERSHIP STYLE

For as many questions a potential boss may ask you about your work history, be prepared to interview them about how they handle certain workplace dynamics and team structures. The initial interview is like a first dance—you need to let them lead. Please always act like you want the role, even if you feel on the fence about the opportunity. If you're on the fence, you won't get a second chance. In my experience, a potential employer's impression of your lack of interest in the role is the number one reason they will turn you down post interview. If you have questions for them on the first interview, be respectful and wait for the end portion of the interview when they inevitably ask, *"Do you have any questions for me?"*

Assuming they asked you about your leadership competencies and characteristics, I would ask them about theirs: What does it take to succeed working for them? How have they invested in and developed people in the past? Were there any former executives they were especially proud to groom? Do they care about their employees' work-life balance, and do they focus on it for themselves?

HAVE AN ORGANIZED AND CRISP CAREER STRATEGY

When you get interviewed, you should have a very thoughtful and concise explanation of how you've approached your career. Have a complete story of why you've done what you've done up until that point in your career. And describe where you would like to go next with your career trajectory. That story needs to be crisp and amazing, sincere and authentic—what I often refer to candidates as "The three to five minute story of you."

You definitely need to have accomplished things that are meaningful to the role for which you're applying, but depending upon how you discuss them, you don't need to have done as much as you would imagine or believe for most roles. Tailor the descriptions of the achievements you choose to include, and be sure they are measurable; include specific data points if possible, like the amount of revenue growth achieved under your leadership. Highlight the attributes that make you a successful candidate for this role. Even if those "wins" aren't directly related to the position, the lessons learned can be.

Are you applying for a leadership position in a marketing company? Your volunteer work to get the most adoptions at your local SPCA may not seem relevant, but it took organizational and leadership skills to put together all of those adoption drives and campaigns to get the word out. Focus on how you achieved your successes and how those skills can be put to use at your new position.

BE CONFIDENT

Confidence is of primary importance after you have demonstrated competence. In my experience it can be hard to find in female candidates. I personally think a lot of it traces back to childhood. Studies have shown some teachers won't even call on girls in a classroom because they want a boy to answer the question—so the girls stop raising their hands. Another famous TED talk by Reshma Saujani, the founder of Girls Who Code suggests that as children, boys are taught to be brave and girls are taught to be perfect. Bottom line is that we need to also teach girls to be fearless.

As described earlier, I was infused with confidence by my father. He instilled in me an "I can do anything" attitude—and to this day I think that is the single best gift you can give to children. Much of confidence is childhood programming, but if was not gifted to you early, I also believe that confidence can be modeled and learned later in life.

You can turn confidence on in an interview setting and really shine, but to be truly confident, you have to practice it and show up that way every day. Doing your homework—reading about the profession, shadowing people working in the profession, following industry professionals on social media—is the best confidence builder. Even for naturally confident people, just being self-assured isn't enough. You have to demonstrate both competence and confidence, and display an understanding of the company's products and mission through preparation.

COMPENSATION

Let's turn our sights to compensation. Even with privacy laws changing in certain states where you don't need to answer the question of your current salary and can't be penalized for discussing your salary with coworkers (according to the U.S. Labor Department Women's Bureau, as of 2019 these states include CA, CO, CT, DC, IL, LA, ME, MI, MN, NH, NJ, NY, OR, and VT), some women don't feel they are earning market rate. How does a woman get past that mindset? To me, it's all about having demonstrated accomplishments—not having reached a certain salary. Demonstrating you've done certain things in your career is what wins you the big salary every time.

Let's use regulatory affairs professionals in FDA-regulated markets like pharmaceutical and medical devices as an example. Being on the front lines in securing one or more FDA approvals and having your name on the submission is the goal—the more of those you have, the higher the compensation you can command. It's a very achievement-oriented thing. For CFOs, the more IPOs or significant financings you've completed for a company definitely elevates your price tag. For a CEO, the successful exits you've had in transitioning a company, either through IPO or sale, with a big win at the end for shareholders is key to earning a higher salary. The accomplishments are what drive your personal market value and annual cash, not vice versa.

As executives, if we all focus on understanding the valued accomplishments within the job category that we aspire to, then we can accurately access the credentials and qualifications which lead to an accurate measurement of our worth. If you are uncertain, ask for advice from multiple mentors or role models in your field. Once you're clear on the rules of the game, you can focus on chalking up these accomplishments, begin checking those boxes off, and see your salary escalate.

GAPS IN WORK HISTORY

So what advice would I give a woman returning to her career as a female executive after temporarily leaving the workforce to raise her children and/or for someone with gaps in their work history? How do you handle this in an interview with confidence?

The nation is currently experiencing a talent crisis across all industries, which will likely be the state of the union for the next 5-10 years. Therefore, the game has changed and even people with career gap histories will be well-received when they come back to the table. It is up to you to be able to explain—in a very concise way—what you've been doing with your time during any gap in your work history. Some people take sabbaticals to recharge their spirit; some take time away to have children. Say it in a factual way and that you're completely ready to be back at work full time—you can't wait, and then explain with confidence why you're qualified.

Treat it like a non-issue and they'll see that it is a non-issue. I have men who have taken time off and come to me in similar circumstances. They've covered it perfectly by not making it into a big production. Men typically have a clear, concise reply and move quickly through the conversation and return the conversation back to their qualifications; they do not apologize but instead explain the circumstances confidently and move on.

During the same time you were raising your children, you may have been doing other things which parallel to tasks in the executive suite, like volunteering, serving on committees or doing non-profit-type work within the school system. Maybe you served as a consultant of some sort to someone involved in a local business or charity? It can be framed as such in this way: *"I have been actively consulting for x number of years. My kids were young and this was the right choice for my family as a whole. I stepped away from the workplace to do this, because I take my career commitments seriously. When I commit fully to a task, either personally or professionally, I do it right."*

Just be prepared when you've been away from the workplace and explain your reasons for the absence in a compelling way. Then, the interviewer will move on.

ACT LIKE YOU WANT THE JOB

In my experience, the most common reason that people fail interviews is that they don't act like they actually want it. It's VERY important to behave like you want the role, even if you don't know for sure. You want to keep your options open, and leave the interviewer wanting to hire you on every occasion, even if you intend to turn them down later. The process of interviewing positively on all occasions is professional, and will serve you well when you find the role you really want.

Let's say you head into an interview, and you've got three or four other offers that you're entertaining and you are very uncertain about this role. If you act too "on the fence" or uncertain, your interviewers will be on the fence about you. You have to really sell yourself every single time—not oversell yourself, but act like you do really want the job. Your mindset should be, *"This is the single best job I've encountered and I hope I get the chance to work here."* If you do well in the interview, you will still have the chance to say "no" later, but when you walk away from an interview, everybody you just spoke with should want you.

Most importantly, if you keep all of your options open post interview, then you get to decide—now you have three or four possibilities and they all want you. This is also a better position to be in during your ultimate negotiation, once you know you're heading into an offer. If you go into any interview telling them you have three or four options and you're not really sure about what to do next, they are not typically inspired to compete, and may lose interest in you. It's fascinating how quickly hiring managers and CEOs lose interest because you didn't show up hungry to join their company. When hiring, teams are trying to decide between two or three really competent, qualified candidates, and they always remember the one who wanted to join their company and who wanted the job the most.

The logic is simple: They want a person who sees this position as a career progression. The role and/or the company makes them excited, and they're going to be onboard for the next three to five years—and they're really jazzed about it, outside of the money. If someone has to be talked into it, it's not their job. Pre-interview, you should prepare three thoughtful reasons for yourself why you want the position. Again, this goes back to doing your homework.

But sitting in front of an interviewer isn't the only time you have to demonstrate you're the right candidate. You up your odds by the behaviors that you exhibit with the recruiter and even the administrative assistant who organizes your interview every single time you interact. Whether that recruiter is with the company or is a recruiter from an outside firm, every single time you show up counts. Every time you talk, you're making an impression.

Ever since I started in sales, I've been a firm advocate that people need to have three or four really good reasons why they make a buying decision, and this applies to deciding upon a new hire too. Since the beginning, this has been the recipe I've used that yielded of all my success in sales. And in this instance, the product is you. If you give someone three or four really good reasons, other than money, why they should hire you and why you want to work for their company, the odds are high that you can close the deal.

But also think to yourself, as you're considering each potential new job, are there at least three really good reasons—money aside— why you *really* want this job? If there are, you need to fight hard for it during the interview. Be careful, however, not to sell yourself too hard, since you don't want to appear desperate; you want to come across as simply sincerely interested and engaged. Money can't be the deciding factor, because if that's the only reason you're excited about the job, the employer will sense this and realize that if you're coming for the money then you'll leave when offered even more money. This presents a risk to your candidacy, so an astute recruiter or hiring manager will always be seeking your motivation beyond the money.

For me, there always has to be a lot of good rationalization— those three good reasons—why I choose to work anywhere. Do I love the person I'd be working for? Is it the right career progression for me? Will I learn various aspects of a business I didn't have access to before? And when I leave there, can I more effectively move on to the next stage in my career?

For the next ten years, we'll be in a candidate-driven market, which means there are more jobs than applicants. This puts you as the candidate "at choice," so don't settle on a job and be sure the employers have a lot to offer you. Your job is where you spend the majority of your time—make sure it's somewhere that helps you to advance your career.

DON'T ACT DESPERATE

Sometimes we see desperate behavior with executives who are between jobs and who are really anxious to find their next role; they've started interviewing too soon, before they are emotionally ready. Typically, they've been laid off or fired unexpectedly. If this is your situation, always tell the truth, but don't bring too much negative emotion to the conversation in spite of how you might be feeling. Instead, when you interview, you can simply say you were let go because of negative business trends and they no longer needed you. Or that your last company had a restructuring and you left on good terms. Assuming this is true, tell the interviewer they can feel free to speak with them because they're going to say good things, and then bring the conversation quickly back to your optimism about the future and how you intend to move forward and make the best of a challenging situation.

The worst way this plays out is if someone comes across as desperate—this is the second most common way to fail an interview. If the first is acting not interested, the second is selling yourself way too hard. Act like you want the role, be enthusiastic about it, know why you'd be great for it, but don't repeat that throughout the entire interview. I often hear employers saying it was clear that a person just wanted a job way too much and therefore could not focus on answering the interview questions appropriately. Overselling yourself is never a good thing and often implies you're covering up other details like career gaps and/or unexplained exits from prior companies. It almost always backfires, I've had people call me up after interviewing a candidate and say, "They sold themselves too much. They're out."

The best way to look interested and show up authentically is to do your homework. Know a lot about the opportunity at hand and the company. Learn from everyone around you—read their website, review all of their publicly available information, listen to annual reports if public, and show up interested to learn more. Have a prepared list of questions for when they turn the conversation back to you again. You don't get to own the first dance—they get to ask all of their questions first, then a good interviewer will ask you what questions you have. The right answer is to break out a written list—it shows preparation and intention to do well during the interview. The incorrect answer is to not have any questions at all, which doesn't send your interviewer a good signal.

Genuine interest isn't overselling or data dumping all of the facts you learned during your research on your interviewer just to impress him or her. I know it sounds infuriating and frustrating, but you'll end up knowing much more about the company than you will actually share. The best way to show your genuine interest is to have a high level of enthusiasm, engagement, and be able to answer all their questions thoroughly and intelligently. This comes with interview preparation and knowing the styles and types of questions that people are always going to ask.

PLEASE DON'T TALK NEGATIVELY OF PAST EMPLOYERS

Be very careful if you've been burned by a former employer. Bitterness is another huge turn-off during interviewing.

Never speak poorly of your past employer, no matter how painful or difficult your tenure with them may have been for you. Instead, you must remain professional at all times and really choose your words carefully. Did they ask you to leave or did you resign? You have to be honest. If they asked you to leave, then have a solid explanation for the reason which is truthful yet shows insight on your part. You need to be honest about what happened. You can reference that personalities didn't mesh, or you couldn't get aligned on strategy, and you and your employer agreed on a peaceful separation. Straightforward, careful choice of words is key.

As a successful female executive professional, I hope that to this point you will have already navigated your career in such a way that you've left every opportunity on your own terms or at least on good terms, even if you've agreed to disagree and separate.

INTERVIEW PREPARATION QUESTIONS

Why are you interested in the opportunity?

You have to really think through the way you're going to answer this. Is it a company whose mission and vision you really relate to? Do you admire the leadership team and their past accomplishments? Don't just say you need the paycheck—that's the opposite of enthusiasm and excitement. The best answer is to describe the reasons this specific role is ideal, and that you really respect the company. Don't say it appears the role was written just for you—it is cliché and sounds rehearsed. Be detailed, thoughtful and sincere in your response.

Why are you interested in making any sort of career change at this time?

When I ask this, people tend to go on and on and on, telling me their whole life story. Instead of doing that, answer their specific question about this point in time and then stop talking. I'll usually later ask for the five-minute "story of you" and that's when you can tell me why you made the choices you did along the way.

What is the five-minute "story of you"?

If someone asks you for a five-minute "story of you," what they're looking for is a logical career progression, aligned with an organized career plan. They want to see you were thoughtful in how you made decisions along your career path. You can start back in high school or college, as long as you tell them a five-minute story that is thoughtful, direct, and quickly connects you to the present point in time. And do not exceed the five minutes! They have many more important questions, and cannot afford to spend 30 minutes of a 45-minute interview on history. You need to get to the present.

Would you be willing to relocate?

Think this one through. My favorite question to ask is "If you need to relocate for the role, who else needs to weigh in on that? What exactly does that involve for you?" Talk through in detail what the process would entail for you—do you need to sell a home, or do you intend to commute? Be specific and don't misrepresent anything. If you really want the role and have cleared it with your family, then tell them you're completely open to relocation—you've already discussed the possibility with your family and they're cool with it. Being able to relocate makes you much more marketable, but their expectation will be that it should happen within 3-6 months versus waiting two years for one of your children to graduate.

Most importantly, don't misrepresent yourself or your family's interests here. If it's a big deal, tell them it's a big deal. Don't sacrifice a whole year of your life because your family has to stay behind while you relocate. Know the answers to the following: *Are you going to have to sell your house? Have you had the house appraised, and are you going to lose money on the house when you sell it? Are your spouse and family really onboard? Will your spouse have to find a new job once relocated? Is his/her job readily able to be relocated?* For instance, I am extremely disappointed to learn—after the fact—that the spouse has a medical practice and a patient base that is difficult to leave behind, or that the spouse is a tenured professor at a local university. Aging parents in the area or leaving the kids' grandparents behind is also a significant consideration to be reckoned with. These are big questions to be thoughtful of for you, your family, and your future employer. If you know the answers to these questions for yourself, then you can talk about relocation honestly and with confidence.

If you are offered this job, what do you expect to earn?

A safe answer is the role's fair market value. If you choose to tell them what you currently earn, that's fine. There's a law now that in certain states employers can't ask for your current salary. It's meant to protect women and prevent inequality in the workplace, but I think it's a mixed bag. It's okay to tell someone if you choose to tell them. If you feel like you're significantly underpaid, you can just say, *"I would like to earn fair market value and what's appropriate to all the people around me at the same level. If this is a vice president-level role, I trust you'll pay me a vice president-level salary. That's not my biggest consideration."*

You do, however, need to also consider money that could be left behind on the table upon exit from your employer. If there's a year-end bonus pending payout by your current employer, but it won't be paid until the following month, then you need to tell them the amount in question, and that it would be important for you to remain in your role until it is paid to you. Give them a start date that allows for you to earn the bonus and to gracefully exit your current employer. You don't want to unsettle them or make them anxious about when you're available. Please note that employers don't like to wait more than 4-6 weeks for you to join, and many need you within 2-3 weeks. Don't tell them your exit timeline is six months—it will be too long, and you will therefore likely miss this career opportunity. Often your new employer can bridge the cash gap for the bonus left behind with a sign-on bonus, but if it is very large, they will have a hard time keeping you whole as you transition.

Cash paybacks to your current employer may apply, particularly if you were relocated for the role and if you leave within a specified timeframe. If you are aware of this situation, you need to disclose that to your recruiter or employer saying something like *"It's been less than a year since my current employer relocated me, so I would need to repay that relocation assistance. Hopefully, my next employer would be willing to help with that."*

This is all a negotiation for later, but you want to register the big items early and remind them once they get serious about you. Holding them in confidence and disclosing immediately before the offer will likely backfire, as some companies simply cannot meet you where you need to be cash-wise. Don't waste their time—or yours—be respectful and share important facts that will later affect your offer.

Do you have any questions for us?

That's the employer wanting to see how relevant your questions are, and essentially asking if you've done your homework. Keep in mind that what you decide to ask also shows what aspects of a job are important to you.

Keep your questions focused on high-level company characteristics, but ask things you actually would like to learn more about. Some good topics are:

- *What can you tell me about the vision of the CEO and his or her communication style?*

- *Please talk with me about the culture of the company, and what it takes to succeed there in an executive level role.*

- *I'd like to learn about the executive team's primary objectives in this year's strategic plan.*

- *How do you explain the drop in share price last month and your expectations for how the stock performance might recover?*

Have a list, but don't overwhelm them; only ask a few specific questions. Keep your eye on the time they have allocated for you.

They may also say, "It seems like you're not perfectly aligned for this position, but we have a lot of jobs here at the company. What would be your ideal role? What's the perfect next step for your career?"

It's very important to have an ideal role in mind to describe. A lot of really successful people will say things to the effect of, "I want to make a difference in the world. That's very important to me. I want to work amongst great people and have good career advancement opportunity. My ideal job involves continued learning and personal growth while working for a company that values diversity. Those are things that are important to me as far as my ideal opportunity goes and they line up with my aspirations."

If we decide you're our candidate and we extend an offer, how quickly can you get here?

As I said before, you want to give them a start date that allows for you to wrap things up with your current employer. The worst answer you can give is that it'll take a long time for you to start. I often get this with academic candidates who have a lot of grant writing processes going on and they're also teaching courses. In most all cases, you need to be prepared to tell your current employer that you'll be leaving in two weeks.

If you are waiting for your child to get out of high school and say you'll be commuting for six to twelve months, the company will have concerns about taking a chance on you. Commuting during your first

6-12 months puts the company at extreme risk because this is when the learning curve for your role is at its steepest. They're also afraid that you could ultimately decide the job is too difficult, and therefore not the right one to move your family for.

Employers want you to be able to hit the ground running with your family in town and your full support system in place. I can't tell you how many companies hire people and lose them because they later choose not to move, so this employer fear is not unfounded. Obviously, if you're having a tough first year and a local opportunity arises, then they will lose you.

Misrepresenting your start date or your relocation commitment is simply not okay. Although commuting might make sense for you, most employers will really struggle with it for the reasons previously discussed.

THE COMPANY'S PERSPECTIVE

Most companies do a very poor job at interviewing. Usually, they put you in front of eight people, all of which ask you the same list of questions. You need to have practiced all of the answers to those questions. If people on the interview team get different answers, then when they're comparing notes afterwards, they will see your inconsistencies. Giving inconsistent answers is another great way to be ruled out during the interview process.

Also, know the interview team will also be reviewing your online presence. What face is your social media persona showing the world? I've seen many candidates ruled out because their personal photos online were not consistent with the executive level image required in the role they applied for. Don't let this happen to you.

CREATE VALUE

Inherently, a lot of women know they have demonstrated incredible amounts of value to their employer. If you know that if you were to leave suddenly, there would be extreme hardship to the company, then you have value. That's not to say you're irreplaceable or that you've worked yourself into a corner, but that you consistently perform in ways that benefit the organization.

When you realize your value, that's the moment people will really listen to you. Once aware, CEOs and everyone on the leadership team will listen to you. You have to become astute at realizing when you've contributed something to them and then you can ask for things that are important to you in return. When you have created value, you can ask for growth opportunities, which—if granted—will result in higher compensation. Importantly, don't simply ask for money. If you ask for growth and career advancement, they should not deny it to you if you have already demonstrated value; if they know and can see it, the company and your manager will know that you will continue to demonstrate even more value to them, so it is wise for them to keep you happy and thriving.

Creating value is doing anything that aligns your contribution with the company's goals and moves the company and shareholders closer to realizing their long-term objectives. No matter how big your company is, if it's public you can read the annual and quarterly reports, listen to quarterly performance calls, and ask your CEO where he or she needs value created in the company this year. As you climb the ladder at work, you want to contribute to projects that move the needle in that direction.

If you don't know what those are, start talking to your boss about the management team's goals and objectives of the company for the year and each particular quarter. Tell the boss you want to make sure that whatever you're working on is aligned with the corporate goals and adding value to that equation. When you start communicating that way to your company, the management team—and ideally the CEO—will know you're on the ball and a key contributor.

Every company, even if it's a non-profit, is about creating value for the shareholders (or donors if a non-profit) and the employees. Make sure your job is adding value. If your job isn't adding value, you need to go to your boss and make a suggestion about how your role can be changed to enhance your contribution to the organization. By doing this, you're creating value in two ways: letting your higher ups know you have an executive mindset and setting yourself up to demonstrate further value over time. This improves your odds of advancing your career.

Take initiative. Go to the commercial department and find out about upcoming product launches. Talk to the head of sales and marketing. Make sure you're working on things you can later demonstrate to your boss as value you have created. Take the time to summarize your accomplishments into bullet points for your resume and your LinkedIn profile under that role. Be as specific as possible and quantify your achievements whenever possible (for instance percentage growth while you were in the role if in sales, or number of product launches if in marketing, and percent market share achieved during your tenure). Executives love to see not only that you create value, but that value creation is always on your mind for the company. And by creating value for the company, you create value for yourself, and ultimately escalate your personal price tag.

Creating value also means acknowledging the value of others. Don't claim responsibility for something that you haven't done independently. It is transparent to future CEOs that will interview you—they know there is a team involved, and that you are overstating your contribution. On the flip side, if someone later claims your achievement as their own, in a meeting or with your superiors, address your concerns with that person directly. It may be unintentional, and they should be willing to credit you because of all of the hard work you put in to make the success possible. See how that conversation goes first before taking more drastic steps, but note the time and date you had this conversation with them.

If the problem persists and is truly causing harm to you or your career, report it to your manager, the CEO, and/or Human Resources. First have a conversation with the person and hopefully it will stop it from continuing. If it happens again, warn the person you're considering involving HR or contacting his or her supervisor. Then, if no change occurs in the problematic behavior, take it up with their manager or with HR, depending on the severity of the problem. Don't let individuals around you take credit for your work—that is simply poor leadership, and if it continues you should definitely resign your position.

Good leaders realize giving credit where it's due is actually the best way to engage, inspire and motivate people. Hopefully you will have a career filled with good, strong leaders that delegate projects to you and applaud your successes in public, ideally to the CEO. The situation above isn't a likely one, but it's good to have a plan in case the circumstance arises.

ASK FOR OPPORTUNITY

Once you have demonstrated value to your employer, you need to have confidence and courage in your abilities. Confidence comes from creating value and being recognized for it. At that point, you can look someone straight in the eye and have a really meaningful conversation about future opportunities for which you can create more value. If you frame your rate limiting factors, for instance leadership training, as things you'd like to solve or work on in order to benefit the company, your employers will be willing to discuss a cooperative approach to getting you the support and training you need. You can't lose.

My mantra is to never get mad at work—staying calm under the worst circumstances is very impressive and is a much more effective way to solve the problem. Walk away and figure out what else you can do—don't try to change others, just reflect upon how changing your own behavior could change the outcome. Look at every difficulty in the workplace as a growth opportunity. Maybe a certain approach was unsuccessful—talk with your mentors, read books, and/ or research a new way and try it. That's why this stage of your career requires introspection and reflection. Building your knowledge and adding to your toolbelt will help you move through your career with confidence.

You can only control your own behavior—so own it. No one is intentionally working against you and no one is trying to hold you back. You're a survivor. You're a winner—exhibit that mindset every day. Then, approach your manager and have a straightforward conversation about what you aspire to do next for your career development. It is very important to have this conversation before doing something drastic like resigning and going elsewhere to seek opportunities.

If the company doesn't have any growth opportunities to offer you at the moment, they should be honest with you. I'd expect to hear something along the lines of, "I'm so sorry—I don't have that opportunity for you right now. Can you please just bear with us while we create that for you, since you are very valuable to us?" Think long and hard about the corporate goals for the year. You may be able to leverage their lack of opportunity into creating a brand new project or business unit for them. But if you haven't told them of your desire for new career opportunities, you shouldn't resign. You should first tell them and give them a chance to respond by giving you a new scope to your role, and/or new projects. Loyalty to your employer is important, especially if they've been consistently supportive of you to this point.

Learn how to have a constructive dialogue with the person you work for. If your direct manager can't help you, tell them that you'd really love to speak to their boss, and try to secure their blessing or invite them to that meeting. A constructive talk, or a really good dialogue assumes there will be input back from the other side. And after that conversation, you will determine if this job and company will be right for the next 3-5 years. All good leaders I've interviewed and worked for care for each individual employee that works for them and understands their employees are individually motivated—they attempt to understand their motivations and work with each employee to customize a plan. If that consideration doesn't exist, you're working in a place with a poor leadership foundation; it's clear the employer isn't listening to your needs, and you should consider going elsewhere.

When you actually ask for opportunity, it can happen in different ways. After knowing you have created value and have worth to the company and your employers, call a meeting with your boss to discuss your ideas. Your annual review is a good time for this since it's a pre-scheduled meeting. Then let him or her know, "I'm just really not challenged right now, but I think I have a solution. I want to continue to learn and grow and develop new strengths while simultaneously creating value for you and the company."

It's important to reinforce how much you enjoy working at this company and value everything that you've learned during your time there. When I come to these types of discussions, I have always found it super effective to come with my own proposal about where

I think I could add the most value. Feel free to tell them your aspirations to work at the executive level, and your interest to broaden your scope so you can work toward CEO or any other C-level role in the company.

Refer to the value equation to drive home the point that your proposal will add success to the company. Including a financial analysis to support your ideas is very helpful. It could be anything from starting a new project to assisting another team, as long as you have evidence that your new role will add value while being cost effective to implement. Because you've pre-thought your strategy, you can explain how you've developed a successor to replace you as you switch teams or job levels—you've already trained a talented individual who can take over your role and both of you are completely ready for this new opportunity.

When you're exiting a role, or even a company, always coach people on how to replace your position. Have the solution ready and make it easy for all parties. Say, "I want to apply for this other job over in this other department, but I wanted to get your permission to do that. Although I love working with you all, the employees I have trained are ready to take the baton from me. You're going to be fine."

Plan everything, including your succession plan, in great detail. They can't be upset with you, because you have everything taken care of and they will not suffer. If your manager becomes upset, they don't have your best interest in mind. He/she is worrying about their own personal situation and the way they will suffer in your absence. It should serve as confirmation that this is not the type of leader you want to work for.

As long as you're learning, growing, and performing, there's no such thing as asking "too many times" for new opportunities. If you're still progressing and delivering value, there's nothing wrong with seeking out more, new, and continued challenges. If they already know you're a high performer, they'll keep providing more challenging growth opportunities. They won't hold you in a department or position when you've learned and contributed all you can there. If they do, instead of getting frustrated or upset, go to outside resources for mentors or talk to search professionals to see what else is available. These are the moves competent women make all the time in their careers. I did that every single time I changed jobs along my own career path. I made my own proposal, created my own job, and moved myself into it when possible, and was willing to resign when it wasn't.

If you want to advance all the way to CEO, then you will have to learn the full spectrum of functional areas in the company eventually—start now. For that reason, don't be afraid to leapfrog into different departments. If you have changed roles many times within a company, hiring managers won't view this as a negative. In fact, if you explain your aspirations and desire to build broad operating knowledge, they will see that every step you've taken has been strategically planned and executed.

COMMUNICATE

We had a really difficult leadership paradigm at my first startup company. I observed the CEO having a revolving door of talent at the top; he was hiring the best of the best, but frustrating them by not allowing them to do what they knew would be best.

This leader was exhibiting classic micromanaging behavior and unfortunately this happens a lot in young startups. Because he didn't trust easily, the CEO wanted to control every decision but didn't have all the facts and information.

I had been recruited to the San Francisco Bay-area for the role. Given the high cost of relocation and living, it was a risky move, but I felt I was ready for it. I am an overachieving woman who didn't (and still doesn't) want to fall into the trap of poor communication with my leader. I knew how to commercialize novel products but once we began working closely together, I felt I couldn't explain myself effectively to the CEO and he continued to micromanage me and the entire executive team.

"I'm going to read every book I can about this and figure out what I am doing wrong," I decided. *"I clearly can't get my point across to the CEO. What can I do to change this?"*

This led me to read all kinds of amazing books like *Hardball for*

Women, Good to Great, The Effective Executive, and as many books as I could that year; I didn't want any of my success to be thwarted because I couldn't explain myself properly.

But it still happened—I had a very frustrating conversation with the CEO where we differed in our perspective on launch strategy, and I resigned my position on the spot after one year in the role. It surprised us both, but having done all I could in the background to resolve our communication problem, I definitely felt it wasn't salvageable.

Quitting was difficult. It had taken a lot of courage for me to resign; I didn't have a new role lined up and I had a very high-priced home I had to continue to finance. The human resources leader would not give up on me, and continued speaking with me post-exit, since she knew I was right, and it was a recurrent theme with other executive leaders—I was just braver than most and took a position in the interest of the entire executive team. Three months post resignation, I received a phone call from the Chairman requesting me to come and see him. Given my difficult exit and the fact that I was only now recovering, returning wasn't on my list of priorities.

"We're thinking about replacing the CEO," the Chairman confided, "and I'm thinking about taking the job."

Suddenly, things had changed and I was intrigued; the Chairman was a really impressive person. After he took over the job, I agreed to return for two more years.

Having the courage to say, "It's not working" and be able to lay down your job is a big step, but sometimes a necessary one after you've tried every other way to solve things. Often, executives I coach will come to me in extreme frustration with their board or the leadership team.

"Have you told them?" I ask. "They deserve to know if it's that bad before you just leave and go somewhere else. In the interest of your own career and others at the company, you need to explain to them."

Ninety-nine percent of the time, the executive I'm coaching hasn't spoken with his CEO or the board. If you are prepared to resign if things cannot be solved, then give them the courtesy of trying to address your issues before you resign. I believe your employer deserves this and it ultimately makes your exit easier for both parties; particularly if they cannot solve it, your exit will not come as a surprise.

When you experience this sort of challenge, a committed employee typically has a lot of solitary introspection, coupled with sharing the scenario with advisors outside your company that you can speak with in confidence. At this point, actually having the conversation with your company should be straightforward: you've already done the thinking with your trusted advisors and mentors. When the time is right to approach your manager, I suggest you couch it this way: "I really love working here and I would really love to be able to continue working here, but this is what I'm experiencing right now."

In my case, the company actually addressed the problem by replacing the CEO. Trust me—CEO replacements are more common than you think, and may be being planned in the background. Your conversation, assuming you have added extreme value, may end up being the straw that breaks the camel's back. This was an extreme example, however it taught me so much. I kept thinking I could change myself to fix the situation, and I learned that sometimes leaders need to be replaced. I became a student of leadership from that point forward.

The unfortunate reality is that these conversations only work if you have leverage—if you've already created value. For women, it can be hard to understand this inflection point, since they often undervalue their contribution. This, in turn, makes it difficult for women to discuss things like fair compensation and career advancement in general.

WORK YOURSELF OUT OF A JOB (WHILE TRAINING YOUR REPLACEMENTS)

Sometimes it is better to exit your current job and spend all of your time looking for your next opportunity. You have a clear mind, and you have energy to interview. Often, when you're still employed, it's very hard to put your heart and soul into interviewing because you're stretched thin and still not convinced you really need to make a move. You're always balancing the new possibilities against your current role. It's a lot easier to get your next job if you're already a free agent, but you don't want to remain that way too long.

When you resign a position, it is ideal to have a succession strategy in place. Ideally, you've been preparing someone to take over your role to allow you to transition out of the company gracefully. If you've made the determination that a company is not serving you well and you've had conversations with them but they cannot find a mutually agreeable solution, then I would use the next two to four months to prepare your departure. This way, you'll leave on great terms, be able to keep those colleagues in your network, and garner their support by providing you with solid, positive references.

I've personally made all of my career transitions using this technique. The employer gets the benefit of a qualified replacement trained by me, they understand why you're leaving, and no one has bad feelings about your transition. The feeling at the end should be that you left for a new growth opportunity. As I always tell my team, nobody stays forever, and people will be here as long as they are growing and developing as employees.

Unfortunately, I've observed many executives leave organizations in a big, explosive way—I see it all the time and it's a real shame. After working for a company and making that time investment, you should be able to leave professionally while retaining your former colleagues and your boss in your network and feeling proud of the work that you did for them. When the people you've worked with still respect and appreciate the contribution you made to their organization, you're navigating your career with a high-level of integrity, and you're creating a positive reputation that will follow you along your career path. Remember, as long as you leave for personal reasons, which includes career growth, and it's clearly established that the same growth would not be available to you in your current company, then everyone should understand.

However, there are instances where you don't have the luxury of a dignified, professional exit. Sometimes, you're working in an industry where the minute you have that conversation, the employer escorts you from the building. It happened to me when hired by a competing biotech company towards the beginning of my career. In certain environments, it's a corporate requirement when you go to a competitor. It's not usually intended to be negative to you or a statement about your time there, so try not to take it personally if the corporate policy dictates that style of exit; instead, retouch the bases of the personal relationships and explain your choice to those you care about. As I mentioned earlier, I remain friends with all the people involved with that company, and preserved a very special relationship with my boss who was required to escort me from the building that day.

> **An important note:** In an environment where it's standard corporate policy to walk you out the minute you give them notice, *do not take anything with you, and most importantly do not copy any computer files.* When we leave a job, many of us may feel like we created some materials, PowerPoint presentations or other types of documents, that we want to preserve and take with us. Unfortunately, it is illegal since these are the property of your employer, and there are legal ramifications for those sort of actions.

Recently we made an offer to an executive leader who accepted the offer, resigned her current role, and her former employer learned that she had accepted a C-level position at a competitor. Her former employer sued her for copying electronic documents she believed to be hers. In one fell swoop, she lost both the new job and her old job. I caution all executives: *do not take anything with you.* Better to be safe than sorry—the consequences can be very significant, especially to your career.

This isn't meant to scare you but rather instill within you the desire to cultivate intimate knowledge of business protocol—if you leave each of your positions knowing you followed all procedures with grace and poise, you'll have a clear conscience and a clear path to your next challenge.

ACTION ITEMS:

- **Take the call:** Return recruiter calls and leverage the opportunity to network toward your career aspirations, regardless of whether the role they have is right for you.

- **Do your homework:** Draft a list of questions to ask the hiring manager, but hold them until you are asked.

- **Practice your answers:** Prepare yourself to confidently answer the top interview questions.

- **Emote confidence:** Know as much as possible about the company history, competitive landscape, and role.

- **Act interested:** Even if the role is not ideal, interview as if you really want the job—you won't get a second chance if you're on the fence.

- **Practice your "Five-Minute Story":** Include a clear, crisp career plan and value creation events or accomplishments in each role.

- **Explain your gaps:** Prepare concise discussion synchronized with your career goals and move on.

- **Focus on value vs. compensation:** Share the value you've created in past and will create for them in the future. Request fair market value for someone with your accomplishments when asked about your compensation requirements.

- **Share your motivators:** Clearly explain the value you will bring the employer, why you want the job, and at least three great reasons why you are perfect for them.

- **Be honest:** Never misrepresent your financial requirements, timing to resignation, or relocation complexity to either a recruiter or your prospective employer.

- **Plan your resignation:** Thank them for the experience and include your recommendations for how your employer can efficiently handle your transition.

NEXT LEVEL LEADERSHIP

*Learn to listen to the voice within yourself.
Your body and mind will become clear
and you will realize the unity of all things.*

Dogen Zenji

IS BEING A CEO THE RIGHT CHOICE FOR YOU?

Do I want to be CEO? What's it all about? Some people don't appreciate that the role of CEO can be a thankless, lonely job. You need to be able to do three things: identify and hire amazing people, and empower your employees to do their jobs well. And honestly, that is your whole job.

If you prefer to work in a "hands-on" capacity, you may be better served in a different role. Your job as a CEO is essentially to be a really amazing leader of a company composed of a collection of amazing people.

For the majority of my career, I thought I never wanted to be a CEO. On a daily basis, I would travel with the CEO and say to myself, "That's not for me." Much later, when I went into the executive search business, I realized I wouldn't be entirely happy in this field unless I created my own company. Given the challenges of the role, it's best to have a strong motivation to run your own company—you should ideally seek out a CEO role because you have a vision to create something new or because you could lead better than others you have observed in the role.

On Wall Street, female-led companies actually perform better financially—women are known to be exceptional team builders and empathetic, inspirational leaders. And why shouldn't we be CEOs? We have natural advantages—we just need to own and further develop them.

Follow your inner voice, which will lead you to your passion place. Enjoy the ride!

CONCLUSION

Women are less likely to take risks and make aggressive moves to escalate their careers, whereas men seem to do so quite easily.

But why shouldn't women change that? You spend most of your life at work, so why settle for something you don't love?

The primary aspiration for my company—the reason I started my own company—was my passion to change the practice of medicine by quickly finding the best people to accelerate the development of new discoveries for treating cancer and other serious diseases, and to thereby leave the world a better place.

Having made great strides there, my future is committed to empowering women worldwide to find their calling and to realize their dreams. Today, I feel like we have just scratched the surface of what is possible, and we are just coming into our power. There's so much more good work to be done by all of us. And as long I'm still delivering value in my lifetime, I'm going to keep creating it and living the dream.

Please strive to keep creating value, too, in all of the ways that matter to you personally. Collectively, WE CAN leave the world a better place!

EPILOGUE

A LOOK TOWARD THE FUTURE

Women are the key to bridging the diversity gap in the workplace. There have been questions predominantly focusing on hiring and promoting women without focusing on other diverse groups; but when you really think about it, women are already a vastly diverse population. By hiring more women, we will be able to expand diversity beyond gender and encompass age, sexual orientation, and ethnicity as well.

In a time when workplace diversity initiatives are struggling, my company Toft Group—a leading life sciences executive search firm—is committed to building a more diverse, representative workforce. We truly believe that hiring more women is the bridge to diversity. More than 40 percent of candidates we placed in 2018 are women, and we aim to raise that number in 2019.

While I applaud the passing of California's board seat bill to increase the number of women in the boardroom, I wish this kind of common-sense progress didn't have to be legislated.

Executives need to focus on hiring outside of their networks to encompass a more diverse talent pool. The vast majority of corporate directors rely upon word of mouth and personal networking to identify the candidate pool for a new board member, according to a National Association of Corporate Directors survey. It's no surprise then that these candidate pools are mostly composed of men because 1) most boards are already staffed by men, and their networks tend to be their peers (also men) and 2) public companies typically seek public company experience—where the majority of these experienced executives tend to be—you guessed it—men.

But hiring women at the executive and board levels isn't just about checking boxes for diversity; it's about creating a stronger, more competitive workforce. According to research from McKinsey & Company, published in January 2018, gender diversity on executive teams is correlated with both profitability and value creation.

Female leaders are not only seen as more compassionate and empathetic than their male counterparts, they also scored higher than men in a study conducted at the BI Norwegian Business School that measured personality traits of managers, work motivation and organizational commitment. The study concluded that women are better suited for leadership than their male colleagues when it comes to clarity, innovation, and support.

In 2019 and beyond, I believe more CEOs will recognize the industry's and their own failings in making diversity a priority and will not rest on limited approaches to recruiting talent. They'll also recognize and embrace the competitive advantages of making diversity a priority in the workplace. I think we'll see companies implement new, creative strategies to hiring and retaining women and other marginalized groups.

I am very much looking forward to the rise of women in the workplace and all the business benefits that stem from it. This will be the year of the female executive.

Thank you for taking your time to read my book. I would love to hear from you at www.robintoft.com.

APPENDIX

WE CAN EXECUTIVE SELF ASSESSMENT

	CONFIDENT YES	UNCERTAIN	CLEAR GAP
CAREER HISTORY			
Do you feel you're working in your ideal career, and that work is your passion?	1	2	3
Can you clearly state your ideal career aspiration 5 years from now (both role and type of company), and why do you choose it?	1	2	3
Can you easily detail the characteristics of your ideal job and company?	1	2	3
Does your career progression to date align with your ideal career, and have consistent level progression without gaps?	1	2	3
Are both your resume and social media sites up to date at all times?	1	2	3
Can you clearly explain the "story of you" in 5 minutes and with (1) what you learned in each role (2) your reason for leaving (3) why you chose the next role?	1	2	3
Are you prepared to explain gaps and detours so that they are non-issues with hiring managers upon interview?	1	2	3
Are the companies you have worked for considered impressive to executives within your ideal industry?	1	2	3
Have you been employed by each company at least 2 years, and no more than 10 years?	1	2	3
Have you been both strategic and tactical in how you've approached your career development and past achievements?	1	2	3
CONFIDENCE			
Will you apply for a new job if you meet only 50% of the requirements?	1	2	3
Do you research companies that you have applied to, and are you always prepared to answer why you're interested to work there?	1	2	3
Have you left all of your former employers on good terms, and your former bosses would endorse you?	1	2	3
Can you confidently provide an employer at least 6 professional references from the past 2 roles, including 2 managers, 2 peers, and 2 direct reports?	1	2	3

	1	2	3
Do you show up at each interview as if you really want the job, even when you're uncertain?	1	2	3
If applicable, is your family supportive of your career aspirations, and willing to support your journey?	1	2	3
COMPETENCE			
Do you have impressive credentials from impressive universities?	1	2	3
Have you earned an advanced degree(s)?	1	2	3
Have you created high value for your current employer?	1	2	3
Have you asked your manager for more responsibility with each value creation event of the past, and were you granted it?	1	2	3
Do you have a history of earning more career scope and compensation?	1	2	3
Can you list the top 3 accomplishments you are most proud of throughout your career, and why?	1	2	3
Does your resume and social media page include specific and clear description of accomplishments that only you can claim?	1	2	3
Do you know how to discuss your past accomplishments and make them relevant to securing your ideal next role?	1	2	3
Are you aware of typical interview questions at the executive level, and have you prepared in advance to address them?	1	2	3
EXECUTIVE PRESENCE			
Do you take pride and feel confident in your professional appearance, including your clothing, hair/make-up, fitness and weight, executive accessories, etc.?	1	2	3
Does your social media presence depict your ideal professional image?	1	2	3
Do you exercise daily, even when traveling?	1	2	3
Are you often told by others that you present yourself with high energy?	1	2	3
Do you have experience serving on an executive team?	1	2	3
Do you have experience presenting your findings to CEO and/or executive team?	1	2	3

Question	1	2	3
Do you have Board of Director experience (even in a non-profit)?	1	2	3
Have you had public speaking and/or media training?	1	2	3
In a team setting, do you listen more than you talk?	1	2	3
LEADERSHIP			
Do you have the ability to command a room by listening and synthesizing a problem the team is struggling with?	1	2	3
Are you a solutions finder vs. one who simply reports the problem to your manager?	1	2	3
Do you have team leadership experience?	1	2	3
Have you built, engaged, and inspired a team?	1	2	3
Do people enjoy working for you and have they given you positive 360 feedback?	1	2	3
Have your employees followed you from one role and company to the next?	1	2	3
Can you list specific examples when you have engaged and empowered individuals?	1	2	3
Can you list specific example(s) when a team you led out-performed expectations?	1	2	3
Have you attended leadership training programs in past 2 years?	1	2	3
Have you served in the military and/or participated in competitive sports?	1	2	3
GROWTH POTENTIAL			
Are you a growth minded (vs. fixed minded) person, and do you know how to spot the difference?	1	2	3
Do you have a history of consistent, strong academic achievements (high scores)?	1	2	3
Have you earned awards and accolades for your achievements, and have you listed them on your resume/social media page?	1	2	3
Have you been identified by your current employer as high potential talent?	1	2	3
Have you pursued continuing education in your field of choice in past 2 years?	1	2	3
Do you consider yourself balanced?	1	2	3

	1	2	3
Have you consistently participated in outside activities that broaden your experience and focus? For instance art, music, competitive sports, raising a family, etc.?	1	2	3
Do you participate in cross-industry peer groups to broaden your circle of influence?	1	2	3
PERSONAL COMMITMENT TO CAREER DEVELOPMENT			
Have you written a detailed career map, including your past roles and future aspirations?	1	2	3
On your map, do you understand what steps are required to move you from point A to Z?	1	2	3
Do you have an annual career plan that you review at least quarterly to track progress?	1	2	3
Have you reviewed your career plan with your current employer?	1	2	3
Does your current employer have a career progression opportunity in place for you, and are you clear on how to earn the next advance?	1	2	3
Have you formally scheduled 6-10 hours per week for planning for career advancement and professional success?	1	2	3
Do you attend at least one networking event each week?	1	2	3
Have you attended continuing education in your area of interest in past year?	1	2	3
Do you have a list of at least 5 companies for which you would add value, and would aspire to work in the future?	1	2	3
Do you know at least 3 executive recruiters in your industry by name, and will they take your call?	1	2	3
Do you have at least 3 mentors in your ideal career's industry, who are more senior than you?	1	2	3

For each: 1 = 1 point, 2 = 2 points, 3 = 3 points

Total Score:

60-90 = Career focused and likely to succeed

91-120 = Growth-minded learner, on a path to success

121-150 = Progressing in the right direction

150- 190 = Lots to learn, but with commitment will succeed

Visit www.robintoft.com/tools for a downloadable copy of this Executive Self-Assessment.

ABOUT THE AUTHOR

Robin Toft is the Founder and CEO of Toft Group Executive Search, where she combines deep inside knowledge of the life science industry with a passion for building game-changing management teams. In her 10-plus years in the executive search industry, Robin has placed more than 500 executives at innovation-led companies in biotechnology, pharmaceuticals, diagnostics, medical devices, life science tools and digital health. A champion of diverse executive teams, Robin has built a reputation for recruiting women and minorities into top roles, and helping the life science industry overcome unconscious bias in hiring.

Prior to founding Toft Group in 2010, Robin served as Managing Director of Sanford Rose Associates – San Francisco, an executive search firm also specializing in life sciences. In joining Sanford Rose in 2006, Robin essentially launched a second career following more than two decades as a biotech executive. Her prior roles include Senior Vice President of Global Commercial Operations at Roche, Vice President of Virology at Roche, and Executive Vice President of Marketing and Sales at ViroLogic Inc. (now Monogram Biosciences), a San Francisco startup where she was instrumental in the company's first product launches and IPO. Robin also served in a variety of senior management posts at LabCorp, one of the world's largest clinical diagnostic companies, after beginning her career at SmithKline Beecham Clinical Laboratories.

Robin serves on the boards of Scripps Mercy Hospital Foundation, The Clearity Foundation (supporting ovarian cancer patients), and LEAD San Diego, the only organization in greater San Diego dedicated to developing civically engaged leaders.

Additionally, Robin has been active on American Heart Association's "Go Red for Women" executive leadership team and has participated in the annual Susan G. Komen walk to support breast cancer research since 2010. Robin's leadership talents have not gone unnoticed: she was awarded Woman of the Year in San Diego in 2017, in 2018 she was a finalist in Ernst & Young's prestigious Entrepreneur of the Year awards, and she's been honored as a finalist for San Diego Business Journal's "Women Who Mean Business" and "Most Admired CEO" awards in multiple years. Under Robin's leadership, Toft Group was honored as a finalist in the Diversity and Inclusion awards, and received the prestigious Athena Pinnacle Top Company Award.

Robin holds a B.S. in Medical Technology (Clinical Laboratory Science) from Michigan State University and pursued her teaching credential at San Diego State University, later teaching at University of Hawaii.

CPSIA information can be obtained
at www.ICGtesting.com
Printed in the USA
BVHW031407070319
542050BV00002B/2/P